MOUNTBATTEN LIBRARY
Tel: 023 8031 9249

Please return this book no later than the date stamped.
Loans may usually be renewed - in person, by phone,
or via the web OPAC. Failure to renew or return on time
may result in an accumulation of penalty points.

Anchor of H.M.S
VICTORY.

SOUTHSEA
PAST

The Pier, Southsea Common, *c.*1865, from a lithograph by A. Pernet.

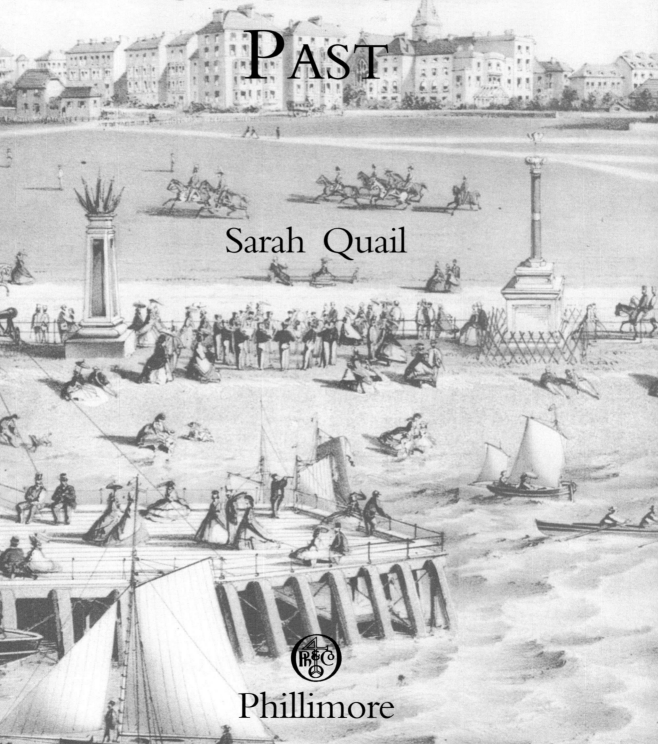

SOUTHSEA PAST

Sarah Quail

Phillimore

2000

Published by
PHILLIMORE & CO. LTD.
Shopwyke Manor Barn, Chichester, West Sussex

ISBN 1 86077 145 9

Printed and bound in Great Britain by
BIDDLES LTD.
Guildford, Surrey

Contents

List of Illustrations

Frontispiece: The Pier, Southsea Common, *c.*1865

Acknowledgements

The author would like to acknowledge first and foremost the work of the many authors of the *Portsmouth Papers* whose efforts since 1968, when the series began, have created a critical mass of original, up-to-date work on the history of Portsmouth which few other cities of comparable size can emulate. She would also like to pay tribute to the men and women whose energy and imagination led to the creation of the series in the first place. The seventieth *Portsmouth Paper* was published in 2000.

The author would also like to thank her colleagues in the Portsmouth City Museums and Records Service who gave much useful advice during the book's preparation in particular Stephen Brooks and John Stedman, and Liz Dunk who produced the typescript. The University of Portsmouth's Photographic Unit copied all the illustrations and took great care of the originals while they were in their custody.

All images used in this publication belong to Portsmouth City Council and are part of the collections of the Museums and Records Service. Profits from the sale of this book will be ploughed back into the care of the collections.

Introduction

Southsea is the seaside suburb of the city—and naval port—of Portsmouth. It is also a sizeable residential suburb in its own right and, although facilities for sea bathing and enjoying marine views existed from the mid–18th century, Southsea developed originally as a residential area: a naval satellite and middle-class outlier of the old town and its original suburb of Portsea. Only later did Southsea develop as, and acquire the trappings of, a Victorian seaside resort.

As the growing suburb's potential as a resort—and money-spinner—became self-evident, towards the end of the 19th century, the successful 'municipalization' of the resort began, culminating in Southsea's hey-day years between the Wars. *Southsea Past* explores the history of Portsmouth's seaside suburb using the wealth of original material in the collections of the City Council's Museums and Records Service. It also discusses the challenges the resort has faced since 1945 and the demise of the traditional seaside holiday.

Chapter One

Early History

The history of the seaside suburb of Southsea is very much part of the general story of Portsmouth. Portsmouth was a thriving dockyard town by the mid-18th century when the first works were published advocating the beneficial effects of sea bathing and a bathing house, Quebec House, was built in Bath Square, Portsmouth in 1754.

The town was founded in the late 12th century by a wealthy Frenchman, Jean de Gisors, drawn to the Portsmouth area by the opportunities it offered for developing trading links between England and Normandy. The great natural harbour sheltered his ships and his new township in the south-west corner of Portsea Island, just inside the harbour mouth, near a deep water channel and the open sea, provided facilities for his ships: quays, warehouses and repair facilities.

There was added advantage—and protection—afforded by the castle at Portchester. The great Roman fortress there had been transformed into a medieval castle earlier in the century, probably towards the end of the reign of Henry I (1100-35). A keep was built in a new, walled-off inner bailey, with a moat, in a corner of the old Roman enclosure which now

1 Lithograph showing *Quebec Hotel*. Advertised on the side of the building are 'Hot and Cold Baths'.

2 Jean de Gisors: stained glass window in Portsmouth Cathedral, *c*.1910.

much of the 12th century they controlled the best part of western France, and Portchester was conveniently placed on the south coast for royal arrivals and departures.

Portsmouth was one of 11 new towns established in Hampshire in the 12th and 13th centuries and conforms very much to the general pattern of new towns established during this time. It was developed on the initiative of the landowner who established a market in the township and encouraged settlers on favourable terms in the hope of securing long-term financial benefits from the prospering burghers and their growing trade in the form of rents and local taxes.

Most of the evidence for the town's early development is recorded in the surviving cartularies of the Austin canons of the former priory at Southwick. The original foundation which followed the rule of St Augustine was established by Henry I in the grounds of Portchester Castle in the 1120s. The priory church, *c*.1130, still stands, little altered, in the Outer Bailey. Today it is Portchester parish church. Within twenty years of the original foundation, however, the canons moved to a new site at Southwick where they remained until their house was dissolved by Henry VIII in his wholesale purge of religious orders in 1438. The cartularies contain copies of documents recording gifts to the priory of land, churches, chapels, houses, shops and tithes. It is here that the earliest references to Portsmouth's founder, Jean de Gisors, occur, most importantly to his purchase of the manor of Buckland from the de Port family, between 1164 and 1177. The manor of Buckland covered the south-western portion of Portsea Island, including the area known today as Old Portsmouth and the site of the new settlement. The cartulary also records Jean de Gisors' gift to Southwick Priory *c*.1180-6 of a site for the erection of a chapel 'in honour of the glorious martyr, Thomas of Canterbury, formerly Archbishop'. Parts of this chapel, the chancel and transepts, still stand today being part of the Anglican Cathedral of

formed an outer bailey. Later in the century Henry II had the keep increased in height and a dungeon built. Between them, the Plantagenet kings of England used Portchester extensively as they entered and left the country because for

St Thomas of Canterbury. A later gift by Jean de Gisors to the canons of Southwick between 1185 and 1194 of a messuage contains the first recorded reference to the place name Portsmouth. The messuage, he noted, was no longer on 'his land called *Sudewede* but in my vill of Portsmouth'.

Jean de Gisors did not enjoy the fruits of his investment for long, however. In 1194 he forfeited all his English possessions, including Portsmouth, when the king, Richard I, returned home from captivity. Richard's capture on his way home overland from the Third Crusade and his subsequent imprisonment by the German Emperor 1192-4 was a splendid excuse for his enemies, the French king, Philippe Auguste and his own brother, Prince John, to unite together to secure their own ends. The French king invaded Richard's Norman possessions, capturing Gisors and besieging Rouen. John, hoping to supplant Richard, raised a rebellion in England and entered into an alliance with Philippe Auguste who began now to prepare for an invasion of England.

Fortunately the energetic intervention of the dowager Queen Eleanor and loyal servants of the king saved the situation. Eleanor extracted oaths of allegiance from the most powerful barons in the land, had the country's defences repaired and reinforced the various garrisons. There was a general muster and a watch kept on the southern coasts which deterred the would-be invaders. John's supporters were besieged in their strongholds and in due course his rebellion petered out. In the meantime negotiations began for Richard's ransom and release. Terms were concluded and, when this news reached England, John fled to France and his partisans dispersed. Their lands were confiscated by the Crown and it is clear from the surviving records that Jean de Gisors' English possessions were among these. 'Portsmouth is an escheat of the lord king and is worth with its belongings £20', one source records. It is not surprising that Jean de Gisors had thrown in his lot with the rebels. Gisors, where he lived for much of the year, was now in the hands of the French king and he had to face the reality that most of his property and

3 Portchester Castle shown here in the late 18th century. The parish church can be made out with its small steeple.

that of his vassals lay now in French territory. Their English possessions were small in comparison, worth probably little more than £100 per annum.

The Crown usually sold on escheated lands, fairly promptly, to the highest bidder. Richard was in dire need of funds, too—to pay the balance of his ransom and to put an army in the field to reclaim his Norman possessions from the French king. And to raise money quickly much of the escheated land of John's former partisans was indeed sold quickly. However, the king did not sell the new town of Portsmouth. He 'retained' the town in his own hands, as the first royal charter of 1194 puts it, influenced no doubt by its strategic importance. Portsmouth occupied a key position on an administrative axis which united the old Norman ducal capital of Rouen with Caen, the seat of the Norman Exchequer and, across the Channel, Winchester where the English Treasury was situated. The English court and departments of state were still essentially itinerant. Only the Treasury had established a permanent home—in Winchester for purely practical reasons. Portsmouth would clearly be an extremely useful link in this chain and Exchequer records do indeed show that many loads of treasure were shipped to Normandy through Portsmouth during Richard's reign. The king must also have been impressed, like Jean de Gisors before him, by Portsmouth's many advantages: the great natural harbour, the shelter afforded by the Isle of Wight, the deep water channel hugging the shore and, no doubt, the quays, warehouses, docking and repair facilities established here already—and free of the straitjacket of any powerful baron or borough court such as existed in Southampton.

And so it was that Richard summoned to Portsmouth in April 1194, at the beginning of the campaigning season, both a fleet and men to begin the great undertaking: the reconquest of Normandy. He joined them there on 25 April. Bad weather delayed their departure for over three weeks. Frustrated, the troops, encamped on the rough ground surrounding the town, squabbled and fought amongst themselves. The king himself was forced to return hurriedly from a hunting expedition in nearby Stansted Forest to restore order. The business of government continued—under canvas—and it was during this enforced stay in the town that the king granted Portsmouth its first royal charter on 2 May 1194. The town was independent now—as a borough—from the county. It had the right to hold a fair annually for 15 days and a weekly market. There was also widespread exemption granted from tolls, suits in the shire court and from a wide variety of other exactions. The burgesses also acquired criminal jurisdiction over their fellow townsfolk. In these respects Portsmouth's charter did not differ from those granted to other towns at this time such as Norwich, Ipswich, Orford, Lincoln, Doncaster, Boroughbridge, Beverley and Gloucester, all of whom paid a good price for similar privileges. However, where it did differ was in the key phrase, 'know that we have retained our Borough of Portsmouth in our hands, with everything pertaining to it ...'. Briefly, nothing should take place in Portsmouth without the king's knowledge. He had no intention of letting control of the town fall into the hands of either a hostile baron or a powerful merchant group who, singly or together, might compromise or threaten the town's new military and naval role.

The surviving records attest to the town's new importance. Exchequer accounts refer to the construction of a royal residence in Portsmouth. Richard's agents also leased building sites to new settlers and a dock was built which in John's reign was strengthened with a strong wall and provided with storehouses. Treasure, troops, 'engines of war' and even Richard's hawks were all transported to Normandy through Portsmouth. Such was the scale of expenditure that a separate account for Portsmouth was set up in the Exchequer. The Southwick Cartularies indicate that a system of local government was soon in place.

Portsmouth prospered during Richard's reign and its medieval history might have been very different but for Richard's premature death in 1199, John's succession and the subsequent loss of Normandy in 1204. Once it became clear that Normandy was unlikely to be recovered, official interest in the town ceased and it was beset with a series of disasters over the next two centuries. It was raided by the barons of the Cinque Ports in 1265 and between 1338 and 1380 there were four hostile raids by French ships. By 1380, the town was apparently all but destroyed. Respite from misfortune really came only in the late 15th century when growing French power persuaded Henry VII that the defences at the harbour mouth needed reinforcement and, in 1495, he ordered the building of a dry dock, in the vicinity of the King's Stairs in the present Naval Base. Large sums of money were spent on the

project and associated workshops and storehouses. Together, as John Webb has said, they formed 'the nucleus of what was to become by the 18th century one of Britain's largest industrial undertakings'. Henry VIII developed the port's facilities further. Brewhouses were built at the top of St Nicholas Street—the *Dragon*, the *Lyon*, the *Whight Hart* and the *Rose*—to supply his ships and in spring 1544, fearful of a French attack on Portsmouth, he ordered work to begin on a new castle to command the deepwater channel into Portsmouth where the ships came closest to the shore. Partly funded by monies raised from the disposal of monastic sites, Southsea Castle was completed in the record time of six months. It was one of a series of forts built along the south coast by Henry who was afraid of a combined invasion by France and Spain in the wake of his conflict with the Pope over his divorce.

4 Southsea Castle: a reconstruction of the Tudor castle by Alan Sorrell.

Southsea Castle is important. Not only is the place-name 'Southsea' recorded now for the first time but the building itself represented a major shift in ideas relating to military engineering. These new ideas originated in Italy and the Eastern Mediterranean and recognised that medieval rounded towers and bastions represented too good a target for modern cannon-fire and provided too little flanking cover. Angled bastions, however, reduced the size of the target and guns sited in the flanks of adjacent angled bastions gave all-round cover. Southsea Castle was therefore built with a square keep, rectangular gun platforms to the east and west and angled bastions on the north and south. It was from these battlements that in the following year, 1545, Henry VIII saw the pride of his fleet, the *Mary Rose*, built in Portsmouth, capsize before a French invading force. Fortunately, the French insurgents failed to make good their advantage.

Fear of invasion from Spain towards the end of the 16th century meant that some efforts were made to keep the town's defences in good repair but as this particular danger receded and the risk of attack from the Spanish Netherlands increased, Portsmouth sank back into relative insignificance once again and naval bases developed on the Thames at Deptford, Woolwich and Chatham. Only war with France again in the mid-17th century would bring about a revival in the town's fortunes.

Southsea Castle's fortunes mirrored those of the town. The castle was sadly neglected in the early 17th century, a Privy Council report in 1623 stating that it was 'verie ill prepared for defence in any occasion that might befall both through the defect of men and munition'. When the keep was gutted by fire in 1627, it was a good eight years before the repairs were put in hand. The Castle did see action during the Civil War, however, even if it was a somewhat inglorious affair. When war broke out in 1642 between the king and Parliament, the governor of Portsmouth, Colonel George Goring, declared for King

Charles. Parliamentary forces led by Colonel Norton of Southwick marched on the town and besieged it. They also threatened to take the Castle which, while it had some 14 guns and assorted small arms, was somewhat disadvantaged by the size of its garrison of only 12 men. There were two troops of Parliamentary cavalry and 400 infantry pitched against this pitiful complement and their drunken commander, Captain Chaloner, when the assault began one Saturday night in September 1642. They capitulated as soon as the first Parliamentary troops had scaled the walls. There was little support for the Royalist cause in Portsmouth and, with the Castle and Gosport in Parliamentary hands, Portsmouth surrendered a few days later and remained loyal to Parliament for both the rest of the war and the Commonwealth period.

It was the long series of wars, against the Dutch in the early years of Charles II's reign and, more importantly, against the French in the late 17th and 18th centuries, which transformed Portsmouth. Early in his reign, Charles II commissioned a major review of the nation's defences and, over a 20-year period, the defences of the most important naval ports and dockyards opposite the coasts of France and the former Spanish Netherlands, the United Provinces, were overhauled and updated. Portsmouth's fortifications were almost entirely rebuilt by Charles' chief military engineer, the Dutch-born Sir Bernard de Gomme, who had served with distinction on the Royalist side during the Civil War. Familiar with advances made in military engineering on the continent where the main emphasis of defence was shifting from the curtain walls of strongholds outwards, beyond the original moat, to a second moat and outworks, de Gomme retained Portsmouth's original line of fortifications but remodelled the ramparts and bastions and gave greater depth to the defences with a second moat and assorted outworks. The dockyard was also enclosed within a simple earthwork and, at Southsea Castle, the defences were

5 The sinking of the *Mary Rose* in 1545 from the 18th-century Cowdray print.

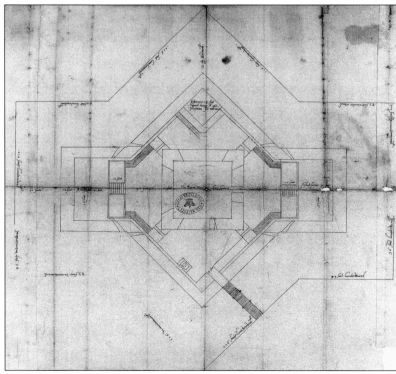

6 Plan of Southsea Castle, 1577.

strengthened with a new gun platform between the Castle and the sea and a dry moat, glacis and covered way on the landward side. A scheme of defensive works was also put in hand on the Gosport side of the harbour where a rampart and moat were constructed to protect the town on the landward side and two small forts were built to help strengthen the defences at the harbour mouth.

The dockyard was increasing in size throughout this period. New plots of land were acquired in 1658, 1663, 1688, 1689, 1723, 1773 and 1790 and, as the dockyard expanded, there came with it the need for more workers, so the local population grew and the development of suburbs began beyond the limited confines of the old fortified town, a cramped existence described vividly by Robert Wilkins in 1748:

The town, consisting of about Six Hundred Houses, is enclosed within a Stone-Wall, several Feet thick and deep; and upon that, a very thick Mud-Wall, as high, or rather higher, than the Tops of the Houses; so that the inhabitants are constantly buried in smoak: But as the greatest part of them are natives of the place, and upon that Account inured to it, they seldom mention it as an inconvenience. They are badly supplied with water, having none but what partakes of a saline Quality; and even this so very scarce, that were it not for showers of Rain, which is most industriously catched by every Body, the people could not possibly subsist.

In the early 18th century houses began to be built outside the town walls on Portsmouth Common, to the north and on the common fields of East and West Dock Fields nearby. The new suburb developed rapidly. By January

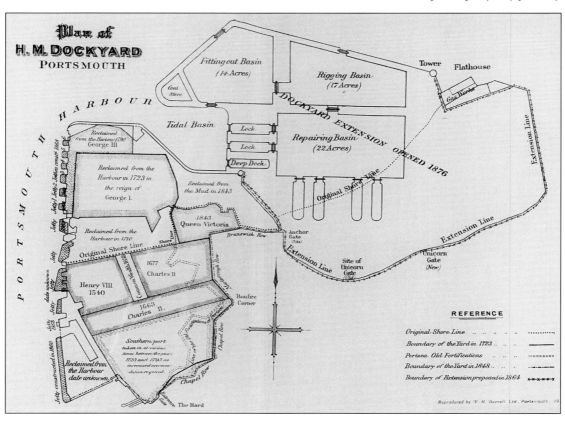

7 Sketch plan of the Dockyard expansion, 1540-1864.

8 Southsea Castle, 1738.

9 Portsmouth as seen from Gosport, 1750.

1728-9, Stephen Martin-Leake, a Clerk in the Navy Pay Office visiting Portsmouth in the course of his duties, noted:

> On the landside, eastward (for their [sic] is none to the south) a little way from the Land Gate, are very large suburbs extending to the dock, and joined by the Ordnance to the Mill Gate, all which taken together is much more than the whole town.

Daniel Defoe also remarked following his visit in 1724 that,

> Since the increase of business at this place, by the long continuance of the war, the confluence of people has been so great, and the town not admitting any enlargement for buildings, that a kind of a suburb, or rather a new town has been built on the healthy ground adjoining to the town, which is so well built, and seems to encrease so fast, that in time it threatens to outdo for numbers of inhabitants, and beauty of buildings, even the town itself ...

Certainly by 1753 there were enough people prepared to raise money to build a church, St George's, a chapel-of-ease to the mother church of St Mary's Portsea, a mile or so away at Kingston. John Wesley, the founder of the Methodist movement who visited Portsmouth in 1753, actually noted that by this time the Common was 'now all turned into streets'. In 1787 a second church, St John's, was constructed. Again, it was a chapel-of-ease to Portsea. The fortification of this new suburb began in 1770. Ramparts encircled the area from the Mill Pond which separated the old town from the new township to the north of the Dockyard itself. Two new gates, the Lion and the Unicorn Gates, gave access. By an Improvement Act of 1792 Portsmouth Common, as the new suburb had been known until now, became the town of Portsea. Despite its new name, however, and the growing size of its population—24,327 by 1801 compared with Portsmouth's 7,829—

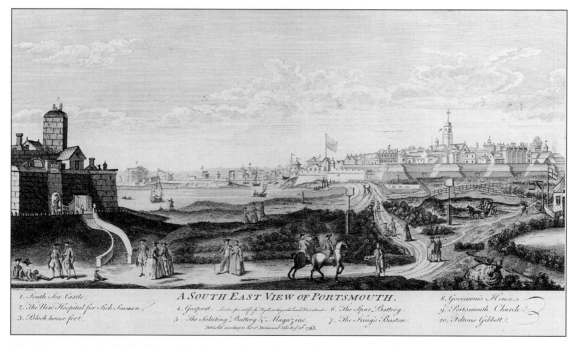

10 Portsmouth in 1765. The original town, behind its walls, is separated from Southsea Castle by the rough terrain which in due course would be developed into the beach, promenade and public rooms of the early resort.

11 Portsmouth Point by Thomas Rowlandson, which depicts famously the depravity deplored by so many
visitors to Portsmouth in the late 18th century.

Portsea never acquired corporate status and
remained always a suburb of the borough of
Portsmouth.

Between them, as a port and garrison
town, Portsmouth and Portsea enjoyed a lively
reputation, the military and naval establishment
presiding over a local population described by
John Wesley in 1753 as 'so civil a people
I never saw before in any seaport town in
England' and by General James Wolfe in 1758
before setting out for Canada as 'diabolical'.
'It is a doubt to me', he told his mother,
'if there is such another collection of demons
upon the whole earth. Vice, however, wears
so ugly a garb that it disgusts rather than
tempts.' Dr. George Pinckard developed this
theme some years later in the autumn of
1795 while waiting for the departure of Sir
Ralph Abercrombie's expedition to the West
Indies:

In respect to streets, houses, markets and traffic,
Portsmouth is not unlike other towns, but
Portsmouth-point, Portsea-common, and some
other parts of the town have peculiarities
which seem to sanction the celebrity the place
has acquired. In some quarters Portsmouth is
not only filthy, and crowded, but crowded
with a class of low and abandoned beings,
who seem to have declared open war
against every habit of common decency and
decorum ... The riotous, drunken, and
immoral scenes of this place, perhaps, exceed
all others. Commonly gross obscenity and
intoxication preserve enough of diffidence to
seek the concealment of night ... but here
hordes of profligate females are seen reeling
in drunkeness, or plying upon the streets in
open day with a broad immodesty which puts
the orb of noon to the blush ...

However, whether they were bemused
or appalled by the activities of Jack on a run
ashore with 'Portsmouth Poll', most visitors to

12 Portsmouth Harbour by Thomas Rowlandson, 1816.

Portsmouth towards the end of the 18th century wanted to see something of the Dockyard and, in due course, HMS *Victory*. As Margaret Hoad has noted, although a bathing house was built on Point in 1753 and there was a theatre in the High Street, 'Portsmouth did not really begin to attract as a seaside holiday resort till after the Napoleonic Wars ... '. Both bathing house and theatre were built for the use of local residents able to afford to patronise such places—the military and naval establishment.

Visitors came to see England's greatest industrial undertaking. The antiquary and naturalist Thomas Pennant, who made a journey through the southern counties of England to the Isle of Wight in 1793, was typical of those who visited the dockyard. The sheer scale of the enterprise impressed him:

The place for the making of anchors was truly a giant's cave: seventy or eighty brawny fellows were amidst the fires busied in fabricating those securities to our shipping ... The ropewalk is not less than eight hundred and seventy feet long. The making a great cable is a wonderful sight; a hundred men are required for the purpose, and the labour is so hard that they cannot work at it more than four hours in the day.

'This precinct [the dockyard]', he noted further, 'contains everything which our navy can want. The vastness of the magazines can scarcely be conceived.'

Joseph Haydn, the Austrian composer and musician who was visiting London at the time, came down to Portsmouth in July 1794 expressly to see the French ships captured by Lord Howe on the Glorious First of June. He was similarly impressed by the dockyard too: 'The Dockyard, or the place where the ships are built is of an enormous size, and has a great many splendid buildings.'

He noted with sadness, however, that he was unable to go inside because he was a foreigner, so he confined his remaining observations to the ships in the harbour and particularly 'the French ship-of-the line called *le just*' which was 'terribly shot to pieces'. An anonymous visitor on a tour of the western counties of England in 1807 did gain admittance. Again, he was mightily impressed by the dockyard:

> a depot of naval stores, truly calculated to impress every visitor with an idea of the power and grandeur of the first maritime nation in the world. The first object of attention, on entering, is the mast-house, where masts of all sizes are ranged in regular order; and some of them being grazed with balls, are suspended as trophies of naval victories. The rope-house above is nearly a quarter of a mile long. Some of the cables require 100 men to work them, whose labour is so hard, that it seldom exceeds four hours a day ...

He marvelled at the ingenuity of the block mills

> where machinery of the most ingenious invention, saws, chips, and shapes the block, drives the whole in the centre, even polishes the iron and brasswork; in a word, performs every operation but that of the last polish, which is given by the hand.

Like Thomas Pennant before him, he was awestruck by the anchor-forge where

> the continued and copious waste of perspiration, occasioned by violent labour, and exposure to the intense heat of the furnaces, requires [the men] to be supplied with five pints of small beer, and with three pints and a half of strong beer daily, which, with wages of 29s per week, form a sufficient inducement to these Cyclops to abridge their life, and to live in the emblem of Tartarus for sixteen hours every day.

By the late 18th century, however, further development had begun to take place outside the fortifications of the towns of Portsmouth and Portsea. To the east of the Portsea fortifications, the district of Landport developed in the area known once as 'Halfway Houses' and named now after the nearest town gate, the Landport Gate. This new suburb grew up either side of the London Road mainly on land which had once been common fields. It was a largely working-class district of narrow streets laid out along the former common field strips although later in the century, as the municipal centre of gravity shifted north-eastwards, away from the old town of Portsmouth, the railway terminus was built here in 1847, shops and offices were constructed in what became the commercial quarter of the town and, in 1890, a splendid new Town Hall was opened by TRH the Prince and Princess of Wales. To the south of this new district, development of a very different sort took place.

Chapter Two

The New Suburb of Southsea

The first references to the suburb of Southsea appear in the Portsea Poor Rate returns for 1790. In 1805 they are brought together in the Gaol Rates as Hambrook Row. At this early date, large parts

13 Portsea Gaol Rate returns for 1805.

of Southsea Common, the former waste of the manor of Fratton, were ill-drained and marshy, clad with scrub and gorse. The Great Morass lay inland of Southsea Castle, reaching as far north as present-day Marmion Road and Albert Road. Efforts were made, only partially successful, to drain it under Enclosure Acts of 1810 and 1817. The Little Morass lay to the east of the town ramparts between Hambrook Row and the sea and was not drained until 1823. Some notion of the terrain before reclamation can be gained from examination of the *South East View of Portsmouth* engraved in 1765. Scrub, gorse, dirt tracks and pools criss-cross the uneven land between Southsea Castle and Portsmouth's ramparts. All early development therefore took place to the north of this area on land once part of the Fratton manorial lands, and divided many years previously into building plots. Anciently, the manorial lands extended over the greater part of modern Southsea northwards as far as Lake Road.

Development took place initially on land owned by Thomas Croxton east of Portsmouth's fortifications and south of today's Kings Road. This small community of artisans' dwellings, known as Croxton Town, formed the core of early Southsea but it was not typical of future development. The influx of dockyard workers, troop movements and naval activity during the Napoleonic Wars did indeed put new pressure on Portsmouth and its satellite suburb of Portsea, but this time the

14

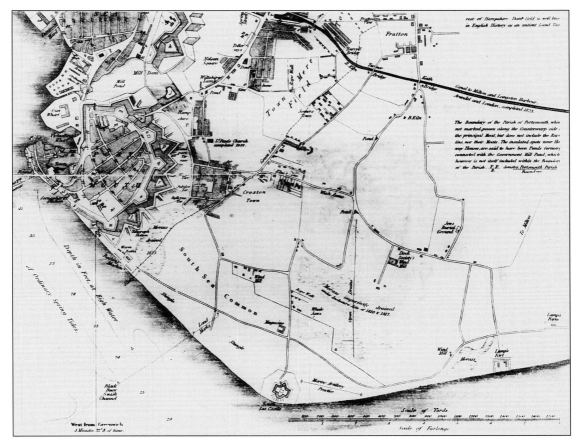

14 Section of a sketch map of Portsmouth, Portsea and the Dockyard including 'the suburbs of the south west part of Portsea Island', 1823.

newcomers replaced the older, wealthier, indigenous population who no longer wished to live cheek by jowl with their neighbours in cramped and increasingly insanitary conditions, with uncertain water supplies and forced to keep garrison hours with all the inconveniences which that involved. They wanted a better quality of life. They removed beyond the ramparts, to the new, more substantial middle-class dwellings rising now in Southsea Place, to the east of Hambrook Row; to Bath Buildings in Wish Street, now King's Road, and especially to the elegant terraces which rose between 1809 and 1812 facing the fortifications: Landport, Hampshire, King's,

Jubilee and Bellevue Terraces. There, with cattle grazing upon the glacis and a row of fine elms on the inner lines, it was quite possible 'to deceive the mind into the belief of its being a fine open park attached to the mansion of a nobleman ...'. By the 1820s, this middle-class outlier, as Ray Riley has called it, was complete. And, by 1830, almost half the nobility and gentry living on Portsea Island had decamped to this new development. Not everyone wished to live in terraces, though, and a number of detached villas began to appear in Wish Street, set in their own grounds. Many were quite large, with fine, uninterrupted views of the sea. A new trend had begun.

There were other attractions now as well. In 1816, the Board of Ordnance had given permission for the erection of a pump room, baths and reading room on Southsea beach, roughly where Clarence Pier stands today. It was the beginning of the development of Southsea as a watering place. There had been bathing machines on Southsea beach since the 1770s, with male and female attendants to assist bathers, in addition to the wooden bathing house in Bath Square with its separate baths and apartments for men and women. There were in fact bathing machines on Southsea beach on the September morning in 1805 when Lord Nelson's barge pushed away from the shore with the Admiral himself on board. Hundreds had gathered there on the Common and on the shingle to watch their hero depart. They gave him three cheers which he returned by waving his hat. It was then, apparently, that he said to Captain Hardy, 'I had their huzzas before. I have their hearts now.'

Lake Allen in his *History of Portsmouth* in 1817 commended the sea bathing along Southsea beach particularly:

> ... the sea covers a fine gravelly bottom to the length of half a mile. There are also convenient bathing machines fitted up and ranged along the shore; as the company which have for late years frequented Southampton, are rapidly diminishing, we may naturally conclude that sea bathing at Portsmouth will increase in proportion; indeed, it is rather a matter of surprise that Southampton should ever have had the preference in this respect to Portsmouth, for surely when the shores are laved by the sea in all its saline strength, it must be preferable to a place like Southampton, where it is mixed with fresh water, and by this means considerably weakened in its sanitary effects on such as bathe for the recovery of the health, strength or spirits.

He developed his theme further, being moved to verse in due course:

15 King's, Jubilee and Bellevue Terraces in 1847 with cattle grazing on the glacis and St Paul's Church in the background.

To young people, and particularly to children, sea bathing is of great importance. Their lax fibres render its tonic powers peculiarly serviceable. It provides their growth, increases their strength, and prevents a variety of diseases incident to childhood.

> Oh, recreation, exquisite to feel,
> The wholesome waters trickle from the head,
> Oft as its saturated locks emerge!
> To feel them lick the hand, and lave the foot!
> And when the playful and luxuriant limb
> Is satiate with pastime, and the man
> Rises refresh'd from the voluptuous flood,
> How rich the pleasure to let zephyr chill,
> And steal the dew-drops from his panting sides!

However he did counsel a measure of caution:

> It is, however, necessary to caution young men against too frequent bathing, and continuing in the water too long: every beneficial purpose is answered by one immersion at a time.

He was clearly much encouraged by the newly-built pumproom. The original enterprise was purchased in 1821 by Henry Hollingsworth who has been described as one of the makers of modern Southsea. He redeveloped the complex to include suites of warm, shower and vapour baths, one for each sex, reading rooms, card rooms, a large assembly room with chandeliers and a 100-foot-long colonnade facing the sea. They were known originally as the Clarence Rooms by gracious permission of HRH the Duke of Clarence who allowed them to be renamed the King's Rooms when in 1830 he became King William IV. As a young man, as a midshipman and naval officer, he knew Portsmouth well and clearly retained affection for the place.

These were still amenities primarily for the local residents, however. Portsmouth was 'a British naval station' first and foremost and a visitor in 1830 would notice first, as did Thomas Roscoe,

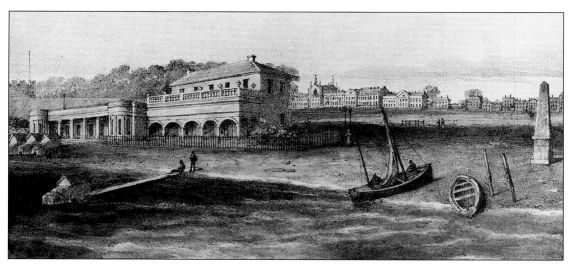

16   The King's Rooms, *c.*1830.

in the forest of sails, the grand roadstead extending into the distance off Spithead, the spacious harbour covered with lordly men-of-war; the fine open shore, the terraced bastions, bristling with arms and the grand public edifices which to the sea-ward at once arrest the eye; all give it that bold and splendid aspect which makes a British naval station ...

He did remark, however, that to the eastward of the terraces at Southsea were:

the squares, streets, and groves, which consti-tute the new watering-place, called Southsea; there is a noble establishment, comprehending baths of every kind called 'the King's Rooms', and from the top of the colonnade is obtained a magnificent view of the sea and harbour ...

And, like Lake Allen, he was impressed by the quality of the sea bathing:

Southsea beach boasts a superiority over any other in the kingdom, for the clear sea-water, and the acknowledged utility which has followed the use of its baths in numerous complaints which bade defiance to medical skill.

He was warm in his praise of both the Board of Ordnance who had allowed this measure of

development and the Borough Council for the improvements carried out, particularly the draining, 'which have rendered Southsea and the vicinity, doubly salubrious, opening delightful promenades in spots where stagnant pools and morasses formerly stood ...'.

Portsea Island's shores were fringed with mudflats and morasses, salt- and fresh-water marshes and deeply-indented creeks and bays: the Ports Creek, Gatcombe Haven, Velder Lake, Eastney Lake and Crana Lake. Gatcombe Haven, a great tidal lake of some 1,200 acres, was reclaimed in the 17th century and became the Great Salterns, but otherwise little of this land was reclaimed before the late 19th and early 20th centuries. Early visitors commented on how Portsmouth seemed, to quote Stephen Martin-Leake in January 1728-9, 'to be in the very water'.

No creeks penetrated the long shingle bank which made up Southsea's southern shore. The marshes lay inland, the Little Morass to the east of Portsmouth's fortifications marking the western limits of the new suburb and the tentacles of the Great Morass reaching out towards its northern limits. Crana Lake could be said to mark the eastern boundaries.

Together, they comprised in 1785 some 180 of the 480 acres that made up the waste of the manor of Fratton, later Southsea Common.

The area was fed by two streams, both in due course diverted below ground. The Little Morass was fed by the Ham Brook which rose in Landport and the Becke-Kynges stream ran from Lake Lane to the Mill Road until the 17th century. The noxious Little Morass was drained in 1823, which works contributed substantially to the success of Mr. Hollingsworth's specula-

tive venture. The Great Morass was a bigger project altogether, its different tentacles reaching out to embrace present areas of Southsea as far apart as Castle Avenue and Albert Road. The 1786 Enclosure Act divided the Great Morass between eight different proprietors with permission to drain but little was done either then or in 1810 or 1817 when further Enclosure Acts were obtained. Only as the speculative builders moved westwards in the late 19th and early 20th centuries did the marsh recede.

17   The town and harbour, *c.*1790.

18   Velder Lake in 1856.

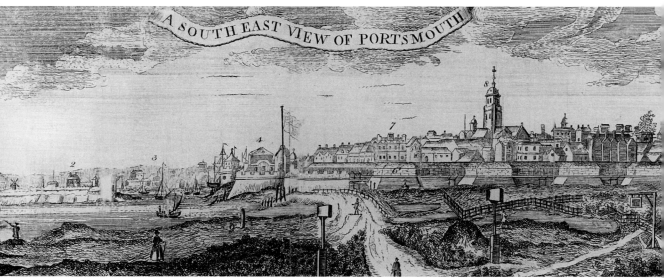

19   South-east view of Portsmouth, *c.*1760

Southsea Common itself was saved from development by the military, who wanted more clear space round Southsea Castle. It was therefore enclosed in 1785 and development was thus confined to a line which marked its northern boundary, so preserving this remarkable open space for recreational use by future generations.

Interestingly, the last fatal duel in England was in fact fought as a result of provocation received at the King's Rooms in May 1845. The challenge was given at a ball and the duel was fought at Browndown between Lieutenant Charles Hawkey of the Royal Marines and Captain Alexander Seton of the 11th Dragoons. Seton was fatally wounded. Hawkey was subsequently tried for murder but the jury found him 'not guilty' in view of the provocation.

Chapter Three

Southsea Develops

Eastward development from Thomas Croxton's lands occured both during and after the Napoleonic Wars. His artisans' dwellings do not survive. The area was destroyed during air raids in the 1939-45 War. However, Park Lane, later Castle Road, and Great Southsea Street have survived and are still essentially Georgian and early Victorian streets of houses for skilled craftsmen and dockyard employees.

Development proceeded in two directions. By the 1840s the new suburb had linked up to the north-east with Landport, along Hyde Park Road and East Street, converging on the Portsmouth Canal, the later railway line. Ray Riley identifies two quite distinct divisions to this 'northern' sector of Southsea: the area between Wish Street and St Paul's Square, King Street and Brougham Terrace, and the area north of there verging on Landport and bounded by Somers Road to the east. This area was made up of terraces of small artisans' dwellings chiefly for dockyard workers fronting onto a bleak gridiron pattern of streets whose monotony was relieved only by the occasional corner shop. The area to the south imbibed more of the spirit of the new suburb of Southsea. There were in fact a number of the local nobility and gentry living here in the terraced housing which sprang up to the north of Wish Street despite

20 Brougham Road, *c.*1910.

21   Elm Grove in 1900.

the fact that, generally speaking, these houses were comparatively humble dwellings compared with the villas of Wish Street and later, Elm Grove, and the grand terraces facing the glacis and tree-lined ramparts of the old town. However, both Brougham and Gloucester Terraces overlooked ornamental gardens and, perhaps more importantly, abutted onto the development which was taking place concurrently south-east of Mr. Croxton's original artisans' dwellings.

This development was much more significant for Southsea as a whole and, as Ray Riley says in his seminal study, gave Southsea its distinctive flavour, socially, economically and architecturally. The area was bounded by a north-westerly line made up of Castle Road, Green Road and Somers Road on one side, Victoria Road and Clarendon Road to the east and the northern boundary of Southsea Common to the south. Development within

these boundaries was quite distinct from the rest of Southsea. There was a striking difference in density to begin with. Large dwelling houses stood in their own grounds with elegant driveways and trees and shrubberies to preserve their privacy. Where houses were more densely packed, as they were on Clarence Parade, they were still a great deal bigger than the houses north of Wish Street. The street pattern was also quite distinctive. The gridiron pattern of straight, narrow streets seen elsewhere on so much of Portsea Island was replaced here with wide and often curved carriageways as in Queen's Crescent and Eastern Villas Road and, to a lesser extent, in Merton Road and Nelson Road.

At the heart of this elegant new development was the first area of purpose-built high quality housing conceived in Portsmouth. Constructed between approximately 1835 and 1860, this area, known today, still, as Owen's Southsea, was the work of one man, Thomas Ellis Owen who, like Henry Hollingsworth a few years earlier, deserves recognition as one of the makers, if not, *the* maker, of modern Southsea.

Thomas Ellis Owen was born in Dublin, the son of a civilian clerk of works employed by the Royal Engineers Department. The family came to Portsmouth in approximately 1820. Little is known of Thomas's early education or early career other than the fact that he trained in London as an architect and surveyor and, at some stage during these formative years, travelled in Italy. We do know, however, that both he and his father were employed on a number of schemes in Portsmouth and southern Hampshire by the 1830s. Jacob designed All Saints' Church in Landport, 1827-8, and Thomas is believed to have worked with his father on the original St George's Church, Waterlooville, 1830, and the first St John the Evangelist Church, Forton, 1831. Father and son, either singly or between them, also designed St Paul's Church, Sarisbury Green, 1836, and St John's Redhill, Rowlands Castle, 1838.

We do know, however, that it was Thomas who designed a scheme for the Portsea Island General Cemetery Company's site at Mile End: an entrance screen, chapel and superintendent's house. His original Gothic design which survives in the City Records Office was turned down. The final scheme in

Grecian Doric was a rather tame work in comparison. Thomas also designed St Mary's Church, Highbury Street, in the old town of Portsmouth in 1838 as a chapel-of-ease of St Thomas's. Nothing survives of either scheme. Mile End Cemetery lies beneath the Continental Ferry Port car parks. St Mary's was swallowed up by the former Power Station site, today a housing development.

Thomas was also responsible in 1843 for the restoration of St Thomas's itself, removing the round chancel arch of 1693 and replacing it with the existing pointed arch. He also put in the lath and plaster-ribbed vaulting in the chancel and installed a heavy blind-arcaded reredos which was removed in a later restoration early in the next century. Between 1843 and 1844 he completely rebuilt the old medieval church of St Mary's Portsea. The new church was not a beautiful building, sharing many of the features of a large barn. It was tall with a clerestoreyed nave and a shallow chancel. Most curious of all, Thomas retained in its original place, alongside the new building, the ancient tower. The whole incongruous edifice was replaced in 1887 by Sir Arthur Blomfield's masterpiece, the present St Mary's. Other, more attractive, church work included a Baptist chapel off Kent Street in Portsea in 1846 and the church he built at his own expense in Southsea, at the heart of his new development, St Jude's Church.

22   *The Cricketers* and Queen's Terrace, *c.*1840.

Concurrently he was busy with a number of commercial schemes. He was engaged by the newly-reformed Town Council in 1836 to prepare a scheme for the reconstruction of the Camber to revive the flagging fortunes of the town's commercial shipping industry. He prepared a scheme for wet and dry docks which, like his scheme for Mile End Cemetery, proved to be too ambitious. He submitted a more modest scheme the following year, however, which was embodied in the 1839 Camber Bill but the scheme was never delivered in its entirety for want of the necessary funds. Another abortive scheme was an early project to bring the railway to Portsmouth. He was joint acting engineer for this proposal with Robert Stephenson, the well-known railway engineer. Thomas also had his own brickworks in due

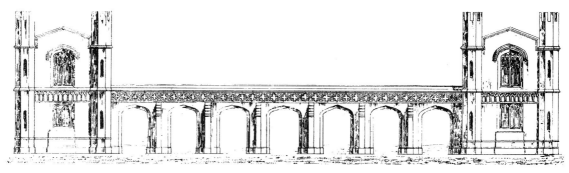

23   Thomas Ellis Owen's original scheme for Mile End Cemetery, 1831.

24   St Mary's Church, Portsmouth, 1853.

25 St Mary's Church, Portsea (1843-87), with its original tower.

26 St Jude's Church, Southsea, *c*.1855.

27   St Jude's Parsonage in Grove Road, 1852.

course which supplied bricks to both his as well as other builders' developments and he supplied piped water to his houses from his spring in Elm Grove after he failed to persuade the United Portsmouth, Portsea and Farlington Waterworks Company to extend their mains to connect his new consumers. He was also in due course Managing Director of the South Hants Banking Company of Portsea by which time he had served some years on the Town Council as a member for St Paul's Ward, becoming mayor in 1847 and an alderman in 1850.

By the time he was elected to the Town Council for the first time, in 1843, his housing schemes were developing apace. This was clearly no haphazard development. By 1838 when he surveyed Portsea Island for the Tithe Commissioners it is evident from the entries in the survey that he and his father had acquired substantial tracts of prime enclosed land with fine views over Southsea Common and the sea to the Isle of Wight beyond. Their land holdings stretched from Castle Road to Crana

Lake, roughly the area round the present Canoe Lake still known today as the Craneswater area.

There is a broad chronological sequence to Thomas's housing developments. Kent Road, Grove Road, Queen's Crescent and Portland Road were built in the 1840s; Clarendon Road, Villiers Road, Eastern Villas Road, Yarborough Road and Pelham Road followed in the 1850s and what was then Eastern Parade, Albany Road, Nelson Road and Merton Road in the 1860s.

Some 106 villas and 54 terraced houses have been identified by Ray Riley as the work of Thomas Ellis Owen. He began modestly in 1834 with Cambrian Cottage and Tremayne Cottage at the top of Grove Road South with combined rateable values of £18. Grove House was built the following year, a much larger dwelling with a rateable value of £45. St Ann's was built in The Thicket in 1836 and in 1837 came Swiss Cottage in Kent Road, now part of Portsmouth High School's portfolio of buildings, and eight of the neighbouring houses in Queen's Terrace on the north side of Kent Road.

There was a lull in Thomas's domestic building operations at this point, perhaps accounted for by preoccupation with the Camber scheme and his various church-building operations. Sussex Place was finished, however, in 1842 to the north of Swiss Cottage and between 1843 and 1845 another 26 properties were built. The following year the monumental Portland Terrace was completed with the staggering rateable value of £639. Ray Riley has suggested in his work on 'The Houses and Inhabitants of Thomas Ellis Owen's Southsea' that this was Thomas's apogee both financially and architecturally.

In 1847, another 13 houses were completed. There was a lull in 1848-9 although Dovercourt, his own home in Kent Road, was completed—today Portsmouth High School's Junior School. Serious building operations began again in 1849, however, and four houses were completed. By 1850 he was thoroughly

back on course again with 11 houses built and in 1851 another nine houses were completed. On the whole, though, the 1850s were quieter years when, on average, only four or five houses were completed each year. Things picked up again in 1860, however, when six houses were completed on Eastern Parade and another five houses there in 1863, shortly after his death. It had been a steady progression westwards on the parcels of land acquired earlier in the century in partnership with his father.

These substantial properties—the formal stuccoed terraces and Italianate villas to the west of Grove Road and Palmerston Road and the informal layout of detached villas in their assorted styles to the east—were tailored admirably to the needs of their first inhabitants. Unlike the old town, they were spacious, well-drained and with an adequate water supply laid on specially. Most of his housing stock Thomas rented out. It was a sound policy. Ray Riley has estimated that the annual gross rental was probably in the region of £4,000 throughout the 1850s.

28 Portland Terrace in 1852.

29 Eastern Parade as viewed from South Parade Pier, *c.*1890.

30 Thomas Ellis Owen's Southsea, from 6-inch O.S., 1856.

Analysis of the 1851 and 1861 Census Returns reveals more about the first inhabitants. Not surprisingly, examination of the occupations of the heads of household reveals that this developing suburb was essentially a satellite of the dockyard and the armed services. In both 1851 and 1861, naval and military officers, both active and retired, accounted for nearly half the households and in some areas, such as Queen's Crescent, for almost all the households.

Interestingly, there is a striking imbalance between males and females living in Owen's houses. Females accounted for 71 per cent of the population total in 1851 and 72 per cent in 1861. There were two main reasons for this. To start with, there was widespread employment of resident female servants (male servants were taxed) but, just as importantly, women out-numbered men within many families because of the custom whereby well-bred young women remained at home until marriage; it is clear from the census returns that large numbers of them never married at all. Ray Riley notes the examples of Mr. H.W. Ross who lived at 5 Portland Terrace, aged 78 and a fund-holder, i.e. he lived off his investments in the Funds. He had four daughters

31 A sketch by J. Calcott of an unspecified Owen villa.

32 Thomas Ellis Owen, d.1862.

living at home aged 41, 39, 26 and 22, a wife still living and four female servants. A few doors away lived Vice-Admiral Henry D. Chadd who had three daughters living at home aged 40, 38 and 33.

Besides the dockyard and armed services sector, another important category of inhabitants, like the family of Mr. Ross, lived off investment income. They are described in the census returns as property owners, fund-holders and annuitants. They constituted almost a quarter of the inhabitants—and most of them were women. The remaining heads of house-hold were made up of professionals such as the clergy, a number of whom were school masters, solicitors and bankers, merchants and manu-facturers—for example, victuallers, drapers, brewers and builders—and finally an 'other services' group made up of lodging-house keepers, providing rooms for elderly fund-holders and naval officers' widows, and school mistresses.

How wealthy was the local population? Ray Riley suggests that some were very wealthy indeed. He uses an equation which relates the population to the sum they paid during 1847-8 in assessed taxes. These were taxes on such items as windows, carriages, riding horses, game duties, men servants and dogs; in short, items which only the wealthy were likely to own in any quantity. Some 49,214 people in Portsmouth paid £18,509 in assessed taxation in 1847-8, i.e. £0.37 per head. This made Portsmouth the fifth wealthiest town in England at this time after Bath (£0.59), Cheltenham (£0.57), Brighton (£0.55) and London (£0.42), and it must be remembered that the inclusion of Portsmouth, Portsea and Landport in these calculations must have depressed significantly the average tax paid by the local population.

Thomas Ellis Owen's houses are not of the first architectural order. Nikolaus Pevsner in his 'Hampshire' volume of *The Buildings of England* describes them as 'odd variants of late Regency or Early Victorian styles'. Sussex Terrace is 'odder than most'. Portland Terrace 'looks a little better' but has 'strangely awkward fenestration' while St Jude's Church shows 'Owen's vagaries in ecclesiastical Gothic dress'. Devastatingly, he finishes his description of this part of Southsea here saying 'there is no archi-tectural reason for continuing any walk further westwards'! This said—and Pevsner was a testy critic—Thomas Ellis Owen's houses are amongst the best local work. They have con-siderable charm and marked out Southsea as a distinctive development from its inception.

Thomas must have been inspired by the work of the great Regency architect John Nash (1752-1835). He was articled in London at the time Nash was carrying out his great works for the Prince Regent: the tall, traditionally-planned terraces, grouped into single, enormous pedimented frontages like Roman palaces with accentuated end blocks, built of brick and stuccoed to give the illusion of stone. There are echoes of all this in Thomas's work, particularly in Portland Terrace, Sussex Terrace, Queen's Terrace, the Eastern Parade houses, and the sadly-neglected terrace opposite South Parade Pier. Perhaps more importantly, Thomas was influenced by Nash's designs for country villas with their emphasis on landscaping which saw fruition in small, detached houses: enlarged rustic or Tudor-style cottages as well as small-scale Italianate villas. The detailing clearly did not worry him. It was the overall effect which mattered.

Other models may well have included J.C. Loudon who published his influential *The Gardener's Magazine* for the first time in 1826. Narrow winding lanes, brick walls, rustic piers as gate posts and imaginative planting were all featured in the magazine and, again, can be traced in the streets and lanes of Thomas Ellis Owen's Southsea.

The Gothic Revival of the 1840s and 1850s only partially informs Thomas's work. His churches and chapels were cheap, often rendered only skin-deep with the now obligatory Gothic style and detailing. St Jude's Church (1851) has scarcely any Gothic detailing at all. Pevsner wrote that the architect of St Jude's was 'a late Georgian builder-architect [who] lived on to learn some of the elementary vocabulary of the Early Victorian Gothic, but hardly the correct grammar'. However, the overall effect of St Jude's is not unpleasing and provides a focal point for the general development.

Thomas Ellis Owen, possibly *the* maker of modern Southsea, was essentially a man of his times. He seized the opportunities presented him as did so many of his generation. He—and his father—saw the sense in acquiring land early in a part of the town which was already being looked upon favourably by the wealthier sections of the local population and he set out to cater for their demands. He did not confine his activities to the housing market. He speculated unashamedly in other fields: in the railways, in banking, and even in the Floating Bridge when the project was launched in 1838. He was concerned with the trade of the borough, with brick building, with his waterworks enterprise. He engaged in philanthropic activities, partly hinted at in his obituary notice. He was certainly a fierce advocate of the introduction of public health legislation. At Robert Rawlinson's inquiry into the state of health of the town in 1851, following the devastating outbreaks of cholera 1848-50, he denounced the intransigence of the Improvement Commissioners for failing to promote a scheme of mains drainage. He is also believed to have been behind the scheme to build the only model artisans' dwellings in Southsea. The Friary still stands, little altered, in Marmion Road, alongside Waitrose's supermarket. He certainly financed the building of St Jude's Church out of his own pocket.

His achievement is summed up succinctly in his obituary notice which appeared in the *Hampshire Telegraph* on 20 December 1832:

> he trusted to his own judgement and foresight, took advantage of the opportunity that was offered, and the result is that the cornfields, meadows, market gardens and marshes of twenty years ago are now covered with picturesque villas and terraces, which contribute largely to our parochial rates, and diminish our local burthens.

Other local builders followed where Thomas Ellis Owen led. Henry Gauntlett, for example, was probably responsible for Clifton, Netley and Richmond Terraces and some infill villa development in the Queen's Crescent area. This was still essentially accommodation for

33   Clifton Terrace and Gladstone House, 1865.

the local population, whose numbers may well have been swollen by the major expansion of the dockyard during the 1840s culminating in the opening of the steam basin on 25 May 1848. What it was not was expansion fuelled by an annual influx of summer visitors. This would come but not yet.

Ray Riley adduces the distribution of lodging houses at this time to support this contention. As late as 1855, a good half of local lodging houses were still in the Regency Terraces, abandoned now by their former wealthy denizens for more attractive habitations to the east. Other lodging houses were located in nearby Croxton Town and the remainder in the roads north of Wish Street. What this meant was that the social and economic pressure from summer visitors was not yet sufficient either to drive present householders eastwards from their seaside homes or to fuel further speculative building development nearer the sea to cater for tourists' specific needs. It is also significant that the first large hotel to be built in Southsea, the *Portland Hotel*, was built by Thomas Ellis Owen at the junction of Kent Road and Palmerston Road, some distance from the sea. It was part of the general

development, as was the construction of St Jude's Church: a facility for the local residents.

There were in fact as yet relatively few facilities to attract summer visitors. Levelling of the Common was completed only in the 1840s and a promenade between the King's Rooms and Southsea Castle was finished in 1848 through the good offices of Lord Frederick Fitzclarence, who became Governor of Portsmouth in 1847 and in whose honour the new roadway was christened the Clarence Esplanade. Lord Frederick may well have played a key role in driving the project forward and, undoubtedly, was the one who was able to organise convict labour for the scheme but, behind the scenes, Thomas Ellis Owen certainly played an important role. A small notebook survives, in his handwriting, recording the receipts and expenditure of the Clarence Esplanade Committee. At the top of the list of subscribers to the project is not Lord Frederick who subscribed only £10 but Thomas Ellis Owen who gave £30. His father, Jacob, gave £5 and, after Thomas, his fellow councillor, Benjamin Bramble, gave most money, £20. Thomas also seems to have been one of the contractors. A small number of statements

34 Thomas Ellis Owen's notebook, in his own hand, which records the names of subscribers who contributed to the cost of the Clarence Esplanade, 1848.

35   The King's Rooms, with the statue of Lord Nelson on the right-hand side of the picture, *c.*1850.

survive recording goods or services supplied for the project including costs 'for sending out and fetching home planks lent for use of the Convicts'. Frederick did, however, present two fine statues—of Wellington and Nelson—to grace the new Esplanade near the King's Rooms and much civic energy was devoted to how best to site them and to mark Lord Frederick's munificence. In due course the 'Clarence Testimonial' was erected by subscription in 1852 at a cost of £300. An elegant column of Portland stone, it was placed 'near the parade ground' opposite King William's Gate. There is no public monument marking Thomas Ellis Owen's role in the making of Southsea but William White wrote in his 1859 *History, Gazetteer and Directory of Hampshire and the Isle of Wight* that he was the man 'to whom Southsea is indebted for many of its improvements and handsome buildings'.

36   The Clarence Memorial and *Pier Hotel* in 1913. The memorial was made of Portland stone and cost £300. It was erected in 1852 opposite King William's Gate.

The Kings' Rooms, Southsea Beach, Hants.

Fitz Clarence Plate Committee

To HENRY HOLLINGSWORTH.

1851
Dec. 26th

Printing

Pd. Spears for Posting and De-
livering Bills _____ ~13/-

Advertisement in United Service
Gazette _____ - 8 6

£1 1 6

37 Henry Hollingsworth's bill for the costs he incurred in raising funds for the Clarence Memorial.

38 Grand Parade in 1870.

39 Green Row in 1870.

The old town was still the unchallenged hub of local affairs and the High Street the main shopping area. Indeed, visitors to the town in the early 1840s were regularly surprised by the quality of the shops here. The top of the High Street was still residential. Thomas Ellis Owen himself lived at No. 16 in the 1830s. Below Peacock Lane, however, the High Street was lined with shops on both sides and the offices or consulting rooms of the legal and medical fraternities. The civic centre was here too in a splendid new town hall opened in 1838 next door to the *Dolphin*. Outhouses and workshops were often to be found at the rear of many of these High Street shops and offices. The major inns and hotels were also to be found here in the High Street and were the centres of local social activity as well as places for the putting down and picking up of the considerable coach traffic. By 1830 there were some twenty shops at the western end of Wish Street catering to the needs of the residents of the new suburb and, by 1847, the number had increased to 42, but they did not pose any serious threat to the position of the old town. Southsea was still essentially the wealthy middle-class residential outlier of the seaport town of Portsmouth.

40 The High Street, 1870.

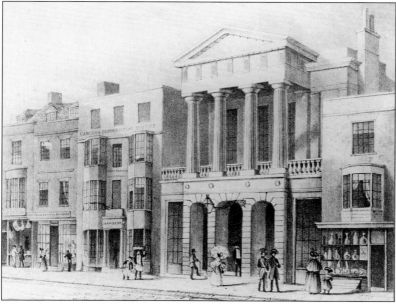

41 The Market House and Guildhall in Portsmouth, *c.*1840.

Chapter Four

The Railway Comes!

The arrival of the railway was probably the most important single factor in the development of Southsea as a resort. Trains—from Brighton—pulled in to the Town Station for the first time on 14 June 1847 on a line which would be operated jointly by the two rival local railway companies: the London, Brighton and South Coast Railway and the London and South Western Railway until their amalgamation in 1923. Trains from the west—from Fareham and Eastleigh—arrived in 1848.

Portsmouth was very late getting its own railway. The massive barrier of Portsdown Hill was a decided obstacle. So too were the town's island site and its ring of defences. It would be necessary to breach the Hilsea Lines and possibly the town's immediate defences as well as build a new bridge—all of which would add considerably to the costs of any railway promoter. The lack of a railway was felt keenly by the local community who resented having to take a trip across the harbour to Gosport to take a train to London once the Gosport Station opened in 1842. This trip added at least an hour to a journey which took long enough anyhow. And if the Floating Bridge was not running, would-be train passengers had to cross the harbour in an open boat, exposed to the elements. More serious was the effect on local trade of the lack of a railway. Edwin Course notes in 'Portsmouth Railways' the speaker at a public meeting in September 1844, reported in the *Hampshire Telegraph*, who demanded to know 'who had heard of Southampton as a port till it got the railway which had enabled her to put Portsmouth in the background? Why should not Portsmouth have her docks as well as Southampton?'.

There was a sizeable railway lobby on the Town Council including Councillor Hopkin, who was solicitor to the promoters of the Direct Line to London, and Councillor Stigant, who was land agent for the Brighton and Chichester (Portsmouth Extension). And of course, there was Thomas Ellis Owen, a councillor now himself who had deposited plans for a Portsmouth Railway line in 1838 under the title of the London and Southampton, Portsmouth Branch Railway with himself and Robert Stephenson as Acting Engineers. They revived their scheme in 1844 but must have abandoned it again soon afterwards for, when the Brighton and Chichester (Portsmouth Extension) Bill reached its committee stage in the House of Commons in June 1845, Thomas Ellis Owen was the first witness called. He said he wanted the line from Chichester to Cosham to go to the Brighton and Chichester Company, the branch from Fareham to Cosham to the London and South Western Railway, and the line from their junction to Portsmouth to be joint. Portsmouth would also gain, he believed, from the two rival companies competing for trade from the travelling public. He did not want to see two lines coming on to Portsea Island and expressed the view that the terminal proposed—on the east side of Union, now

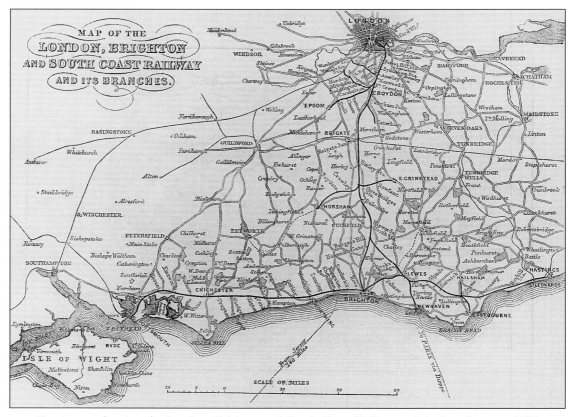

42 A map showing the London, Brighton and South Coast Railway and its branches, pre-1859.

Commercial, Road—was more suitable than that proposed by the rival company. Other witnesses referred to public meetings which had taken place in Portsmouth in support of the bill including one called by the mayor and a petition in the bill's favour signed by 3,000 people.

The bill completed its stages in due course and received the royal assent on 8 August 1845. The line, Chichester to Portsmouth, was constructed almost exactly as proposed on the deposited plans. A moveable bridge was constructed over Portscreek which was still used by craft plying between the upper reaches of Portsmouth and Langstone harbours. The moat was crossed and Hilsea Lines breached through a curtain wall. Thereafter, the line went southwards, to the east of the main road, crossing

minor roads either on the level or beneath newly-constructed road bridges. At Fratton, the line curved sharply westwards and picked up the route of the abandoned Portsmouth and Arundel Canal, terminating in the vicinity of the former canal basin in Union Road.

The arrival of the railway at long last brought dramatic reductions in travel time. It took seven hours to get to London on a mail coach. The journey time was halved now. It took 3 hours 10 minutes travelling via Brighton. Travelling via Eastleigh, the journey took 2 hours 50 minutes. When the Direct Line opened in 1859 linking the London and South Western Railway at Godalming to the London Brighton and South Coast Railway at Havant through Haslemere, the journey time was reduced to 2 hours 15 minutes.

Put briefly, rail travel meant that many more people could travel. Ray Riley has calculated that, by 1870, over 500,000 people were using Portsmouth Station annually. And if we use the yardstick of the number of lodging houses constructed, and their distribution, to measure the development of Southsea as a resort, it is clear that it was now developing apace. Between 1847 and 1855, the number of lodging houses almost trebled in number from 38 to 93. By 1875, there were 195 such establishments and, by 1885, 368. And the location of lodging houses did indeed shift. Between 1855 and 1867 Croxton Town and King Street were abandoned for properties nearer the Common in Osborne Road,

Palmerston Road and Clarence Parade. These were expensive properties with high rateable values. Clearly it was now financially worth-while to turn these properties over to summer visitors. The trend continued after 1867 with a marked concentration of lodging houses emerging in the Osborne Road and Clarence Parade areas. In fact more than half the prop-erties in these and the neighbouring roads were lodging houses by 1885. South Parade developed similarly, as did its near neighbours, Beach Road and St Helen's Park Crescent. Thomas Ellis Owen's Southsea remained immune to these developments, however, the high rateable values of 'his' properties making then unattractive propositions as lodging houses.

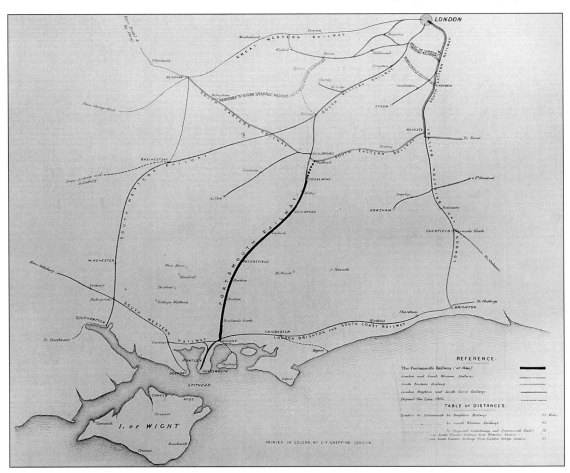

43 Map showing the proposed route of the Direct Railway Line, _c._1853.

44 Osborne Road, *c.*1890.

45 Clarence Parade, *c.*1890.

46 Southsea House and the *Cricketers* Tavern with Southsea Castle in the background, *c.*1840.

47 The *Pier Hotel*, *c.*1910.

Further evidence of Southsea's development as a resort can also be seen now in the opening of specific seaside hotels. The *Queen's Hotel* opened in 1861. It was not purpose-built but the converted—and enlarged—former home of Sir John Morris, Southsea House. Beatrix Potter stayed here on a brief visit to Portsmouth in 1884 with her parents. She was 18 years old and left a lively account of her visit. She described the *Queen's* as comfortable, 'a queer old house with mountainous floors'. She was much diverted on her first evening by the ironclad anchored opposite and the searchlights 'dodging off it round the coast, the sea, and the sky, in a most erratic manner'. The *Pier Hotel* was purpose-built and opened in 1865

48   The *Beach Mansions Hotel*, *c*.1910.

with 60 bedrooms, coffee-, billiard- and dining rooms. Both the *Queen's* and the *Pier Hotel* can be made out on Pernet's watercolour of Southsea in 1867. The *Beach Mansions Hotel* opened in 1866 at the other end of the seafront. Possibly its owners wished quite deliberately to put some distance between their patrons and the comparative hurly-burly of the western end of the resort where initially horse-drawn omnibuses and, from 1863, horse-drawn trams hauled passengers for the Isle of Wight—and

their luggage—from the Town Station to Clarence Pier and the connecting paddle steamers. The *Beach Mansions* was the largest hotel yet built, with 140 rooms. The *Sandringham Hotel* was built in 1871, at the western end of the seafront, at the end of Osborne Road, behind the *Queen's*. It was enlarged in 1880 at the same time as the *Grosvenor Hotel* was rising on the site of the old *Cricketers' Tavern*, one of the earliest Southsea taverns, which stood on the corner of Osborne

Road and Emanuel Road, later Western Parade. The *Esplanade Hotel*, on the site of the old King's Rooms, was the last of the large purpose-built seaside hotels to be constructed in Southsea. The King's Rooms had become derelict by 1865 but were subsequently rebuilt to the impressive designs of architects Davis and Emanuel of Finsbury Circus, London. There was an elegant assembly room some 80 feet long, 40 feet wide and 40 feet high. There were bathing facilities once again, to the west of the assembly room, and facing the sea was a long gravel walk with shelters at either end.

The premises were purchased in 1877 and converted into a hotel. Its two distinctive entrance towers are a feature of photographs and postcards of Clarence Esplanade until the building's destruction during an air raid in the Second World War.

The 1860s also saw the construction of Southsea's first pier, the Clarence Esplanade Pier, near the King's Rooms, in 1861. It was not very far from the Victoria Pier, constructed in 1842 from the old beef landing stage alongside the Square Tower. This was the first such structure of its kind built in the town. It was

49 *Sandringham Hotel, c.1910.*

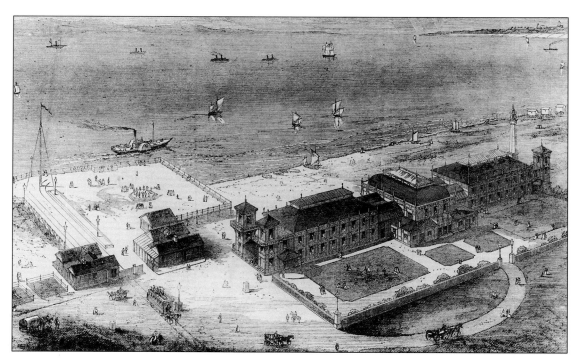

50 *Above left*. The *Esplanade Hotel*, *c*.1880.

51 *Above*. Clarence Pier between the Wars.

52 *Left*. The Tram Terminus at Clarence Pier, after 1880.

primarily a landing place for passenger steamers but became within a short period of time a popular promenade for local residents. As late as 1860 a dividend of 100 per cent was paid to shareholders but it declined rapidly in popularity after Clarence Pier opened. The Albert Pier, built on the Common Hard in 1846, was also used mainly as a landing place—by the Gosport Ferries and other vessels. Consequently the railway companies were obliged to provide an alternative landing stage at the end of the Harbour Station, when they absorbed the Albert Pier Company, for the Portsmouth Waterside Extension Railway which opened for public traffic in 1876 and was in its turn to affect profoundly income from passenger traffic to the Isle of Wight from Clarence Pier, but in 1861 this was still some way off.

The promoters of the Clarence Esplanade Pier, encouraged by the success of the Victoria Pier, hoped to make large sums of money from the tolls they could charge ships' passengers as well as those who wanted to take a turn along the pier and admire the maritime views. Provision was made at the pier-head for two paddle steamers to berth at once. As hoped for, the trade proved lucrative and the Pier Company enlarged the pier in 1869-71, and again in 1874-5. The opening of the Harbour Station did affect profits but clearly not enough to deter the Company from constructing a splendid new pavilion in 1882 for the promenaders and those who came to hear the band play of an afternoon or evening during the season. The Prince and Princess of Wales performed the opening ceremony on the Monday of the third week of August. Ray Riley records that, at the turn of the century, a £10 share was auctioned for £59. Clearly the profits were still worthwhile.

South Parade Pier, opened on 6 July 1879 by minor royalty, Princess Edward of Saxe-Weimar, wife of the Lieutenant Governor, was at the other end of the promenade. It was much longer than Clarence Pier and preserved an air of fashionable exclusivity until comparatively recent times.

In 1853 the *Official Illustrated Guide to the Brighton and South East Railways* described Southsea as 'a cross between a watering-town and a fortified place' and thus effectively underscored what might be better described as Portsmouth's dual role now. Certainly, Southsea had developed—and was developing—as a Victorian seaside resort and was acquiring the trappings of a self-respecting resort but, in its essentials, Portsmouth was a dockyard town, the most important in the British Isles, and, as such, heavily-defended. In fact the 1860s would see a complete reorganisation of Portsmouth's coastal defences dictated by recent dramatic improvements in the range and effectiveness of artillery and growing unease about the military ambitions of the old enemy, France. The legacy survives to this day in the sea forts built of iron and granite on shoals at Spitbank, Horse Sand, No Man's Land and St Helen's and the line of six fortresses along the length of Portsdown Hill:

53 South Parade Pier, *c.*1879.

54 The barracks, *Pier Hotel* and Southsea Terrace between the Wars.

Forts Wallington, Nelson, Southwick, Widley, Purbrook and Farlington. The dockyard itself was extended in 1843-5 and again, 1864-76. The population of the town escalated dramatically. Between 1841 and 1881, it almost doubled from 63,032 in 1841 to 127,989 in 1881.

Southsea continued to expand eastwards but this development was driven by the expansion of the dockyard during these years not by the newly-established resort. New developers attempted to follow where Thomas Ellis Owen had led only a few years before. New Southsea developed east of Victoria Road and some effort was made to build attractive terraces and villas in Campbell Road and Outram Road in and around the hastily-constructed St Bartholomew's Church. Like Thomas Ellis Owen, the developers recognised that a church nearby helped sell houses. The young Rudyard Kipling and his sister, Alice, spent several miserable years in the 1870s in Southsea at Lorne Lodge, Campbell Road, left by their parents who were abroad to be cared for by a retired naval captain and his ill-tempered wife. Kipling went to Hope House School and the memories of those years left an indelible impression upon him. Many children of naval or army men or colonial administrators serving in far-flung corners of the empire were condemned to a similar fate. With its naval associations, Portsmouth—and particularly Southsea—had more than its share of such fostered children who were educated at the numerous private schools which existed in the town. There are 87 private schools listed in White's 1859 *Directory*, 22 of which were boarding schools. Many of them, not surprisingly, were naval 'crammers'.

Efforts to build properties similar to those in New Southsea south of Albert Road did not prosper apart from some development on Victoria Road South. Basically the pressure on building land—and the possibility of better financial returns—saw a return to what Patricia Haskell has called 'Portsmouth's customary cramped monotony' of 'straight rows of large

or small red-brick houses tailored to the occupants' income'. The artisan terraces which spread eastwards across Somers Road and encircled New Southsea to the north were typical examples of such development, stretching from Margate Road to Bradford Road. The encirclement continued with similar terraces appearing between Victoria Road North and Fawcett Road and extending south to Albert Road.

Nearer the seafront, some infilling took place in middle-class strongholds behind South Parade and a series of roads were constructed west of Thomas Ellis Owen's Dovercourt home, between Elphinstone Road and Emanuel Road. Development also began in the Craneswater area in the late 1870s. Some variety and quality of housing was achieved here but it was never on the same scale achieved by Thomas Ellis Owen half a century earlier.

By the turn of the century, the population of Portsmouth had grown to 190,281. Southsea has reached its physical limits, bounded to the north by the railway line and the line of the old canal, now Goldsmith Avenue, to the east by Eastney and Eastney Road and to the south by the sea. It took barely twenty years for the fields and meadows to be covered with housing: 'that bleakly impressive gridiron', as Ray Riley has described it. North of Albert Road and Highland Road row upon row of artisan terraces now housed the hundreds of dockyard workers and sailors and their families caught up in the race to rearm against a new foe—the Emperor of Germany. Development south of Albert Road was essentially middle-class, ranging from the large brick-built villas of the wealthier sections of local society in Craneswater to the more modest semi-detached dwellings of roads such as Festing Grove where naval and military officers, senior dockyard employees and business and professional people lived.

By 1901, the distribution of lodging houses, hotels and 'seaside' attractions was confined to the area behind the Common and to the west of South Parade Pier and, between

55 Clarence Parade and Palmerston Road between the Wars.

56 Lennox Road and South Parade between the Wars.

57 South Parade and Eastern Villas Road between the Wars.

58   South Parade and the Pier
between the Wars.

59   Southsea Beach, *c.*1895.

60   Clarence Esplanade, *c.*1895.

them, defined the seaside resort of Southsea. Efforts to develop the resort east of South Parade did not succeed, as the promoters of the Southsea Railway discovered to their cost. The line opened in 1885, branching away from Fratton Station in a south-easterly direction to a terminus at Granada Road's junction with Waverley Road. The line never paid its way, however, and was abandoned as war loomed in 1914.

One interesting development which took place towards the end of the century was a decline in the number of lodging houses. Ray Riley has identified a decline from 368 such establishments in 1885 down to 210 in 1907

but against this must be set the opening of a number of small hotels, many of which evolved out of lodging houses. Several of these small hotels stood on Clarence and South Parades.

By the end of the century it could be said that Southsea had come of age as a seaside resort. It enjoyed an enviable reputation for respectability due as much as anything to its proximity to its residential suburbs. As the author of one guide put it:

> Residences occupied by nobility and officers as well as persons of wealth are both in quality and quantity a substantial proof of the excellence of this locale.

61   A self-appointed speaker harangues the crowds on Southsea Beach, 1899.

62   Punch and Judy on Southsea Beach, 1899.

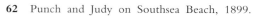

Chapter Five

A Constantly Changing Scene at Sea

One of the great practical advantages which Southsea enjoyed over many other seaside resorts was a constantly changing scene at sea. Daily during the season, visitors could enjoy the prospect of the Royal Navy steaming in and out of harbour. Beatrix Potter gave a most lively account of the ships she saw and visited on her brief stay in Southsea in November 1884. On her first afternoon, she saw the *St Vincent*, *Victory* and *Duke of Wellington* at anchor in the harbour, possibly from Point. The following day she was rowed up harbour to see the *Victory* and wrote in her diary:

> I think this ship was one of the most picturesque sights imaginable, particularly from close under the stairs—looking up at the queer little port-holes, and the end like a quaint carved old house ...

Continuing up harbour she observed the *Duke of Wellington* once again and the *Ant*, used as a training ship for boys. She passed a row of hulks which included the old *Bellerophon* which fought at the Battle of Trafalgar and was used to convey Napoleon to St Helena and in due course went alongside the ironclad, *Glatton* which they boarded and inspected thoroughly. When they got back into their boat, they inspected Portchester Castle and admired the forts on the hill 'whence they can shoot eight miles right over the harbour', reported Beatrix. Heading back they passed the torpedo ship, the *Hecla*, and the ironclad troopship, the *Assistance*. Beatrix also commented on the general bustle and 'no end of small steamers rushing about'. Interestingly for the future, she was also much preoccupied by the dormice she had seen in a bird-shop in the High Street

> ... a most incredible number ... in two cages. I don't believe they were dormice, too large by three or four sizes. Am considering how it would be possible to convey some home.

The dormice were still worrying her when she disembarked at the landing stage at the Harbour Station. She went back to have another look at them, 'Again looked upon those dormice. Would they carry in a biscuit cannister?' Sadly, she noted they were 'grievously afflicted with tickles'.

The tradition of royal visits and reviews of the fleet could be said to have begun in the late 17th century when in 1693 William III visited Portsmouth, viewed the fleet at anchor at Spithead and dined on board ship with Admiral Rook. George III embraced the notion of reviews with typical enthusiasm. He visited Portsmouth on a number of occasions. He spent five days in the town in June 1773, visiting the fleet anchored at Spithead, viewing the Dockyard and the Gunwharf, the brewery, magazines and fortifications. This was the first official review of the fleet. He also made a trip to the Isle of Wight to Sandown Bay, on this occasion on the yacht *Augusta* which, on its return, anchored off the beach at Southsea. At 10.00pm the garrison fired a *feu de joie* from the ramparts by a triple discharge of cannon and muskets after which the *Augusta* made her way into the

63 *Victory* and the *Duke of Wellington* moored mid-stream and, in the foreground, the sort of launch Beatrix Potter would have boarded, *c.*1880.

harbour and the king landed in the dockyard. 'The sea and shores', Lake Allen informed his readers, 'were covered with an innumerable number of vessels and people each day.'

The king came to Portsmouth again on 26 June 1794 to congratulate Lord Howe on his great defeat of the French fleet on the 'glorious 1 June'. With the Queen, Prince Ernest Augustus and two of the young Princesses, he went out in the royal barges to Spithead, went on board the *Queen Charlotte* 'under a salute from the garrison, forts and fleet and, on quitting the ship, went round the fleet'. The following day, the King and Queen held a levée at the Governor's house where the mayor, aldermen and burgesses were presented to their majesties.

More festivities took place, to the delight of the local population and the hundreds of visitors who packed the town, in June 1814. The Prince Regent presided over events on this occasion: the visit of the Allied Sovereigns—the Emperor of Russia and the King of Prussia and their extensive retinues. A series of receptions and special events took place celebrating, somewhat prematurely in retrospect, the end of some twenty years of war against Napoleon and revolutionary France.

For the duration of the visit, Portsmouth became the centre of the kingdom. The town's population increased three-fold and, by the beginning of the week's celebrations, not a spare bed was to be had.

The spectacle was superb. There were illuminations which 'presented a scene of grandeur and delight unknown to Portsmouth' according to Lake Allen. Government House was to be seen to be believed with the word 'Peace' in outsize letters on the front of the building surrounded by stars and laurel. The balcony was festooned with draperies, all surmounted by a star and crown. Everything was picked out in coloured lamps:

> the whole producing a blaze of light and unity of design which astonished and attracted thousands, during the three nights it was exhibited. Indeed no description can convey an idea any way equal to the splendour of the scene.

During the days that followed there was a splendid trip to Spithead to inspect the fleet. As the royal party left the shelter of the harbour there was a 21-gun salute which was picked up and repeated by the ships at anchor. The yards were manned and the crews cheered themselves hoarse. There were receptions and dinners, many in local hotels and inns in the old town. Marshal Blucher himself stayed at the *Crown Inn* where the Prince Regent gave a ball and supper and the Duke of Clarence hosted a breakfast given in honour of the Emperor of Russia and the King and Princes of Prussia, all of whom graced the occasion with their presence.

By this time, a pattern of such visits had been established. The format did not vary greatly during Queen Victoria's reign and those of her immediate descendants, although, of course, as George Wade says in *Naval Reviews at Spithead 1842-45*, 'their social, political

64 Government House, *c.*1812.

and military context changed considerably during her long reign'. The first occasion on which the Queen inspected the fleet was on 28 February 1842. 'Boisterous' weather spoilt the illuminations and it was a small affair compared with later reviews but, nevertheless, the event aroused a lot of interest and the young Queen enchanted the sailors on the ship, the *Queen*, by drinking rum from a mess tin and tasting soup using one of the men's own iron spoons. The men cheered her, the Queen apparently shed a tear and is reported to have said:

> I feel today that I am indeed old Ocean's Youthful Queen, and that I am indeed surrounded by those who will uphold that title in the battle and the breeze.

Between 1842 and 1914 there were, altogether, 18 such reviews. The review on 23 June 1845 was the last review of sailing battleships. It was a splendid occasion in the presence of both Queen Victoria and Prince Albert and watched by an enormous number of spectators on Southsea Common. All the ships made sail and then shortened it bit by bit as though a storm was coming in until they were under close reefed topsails. Only one steam warship was present.

The review on 11 August 1853 reflected the technological change which had taken place in the intervening period. It was the first royal inspection of steam warships at Spithead and attracted quite extraordinary attention. A mimic battle took place between the new steam war vessels and the old sailing ships, which were soundly beaten. The town was overwhelmed with visitors and, according to local newspaper editor, W.G. Gates, himself a naval orphan, 'all through the preceding night, the streets were crowded with hapless visitors in search of a bed'. Another great review of the Fleet took place at the close of the war with Russia, on the fleet's return from the Baltic, on 23 April

65   Queen Victoria goes on board the *Albion* at Spithead, 23 June 1845.

66 Yachts taking out passengers to view the fleet, sketched from Southsea Common, 23 April 1856.

1856. 254 ships of all classes took part, manned by over 50,000 men. Between them, they mustered over 1,000 guns and extended over five miles in two parallel lines. A mock gunboat attack on Southsea Castle formed part of the total display, cut short when the Lieutenant Governor heard he would have to pay for the ammunition. Altogether, it was the greatest naval display ever witnessed up to that time and, according to Gates, 'the town, which was thronged with visitors, gave itself up to the patriotic enjoyment of the occasion'.

Similar reviews took place throughout the 1860s and 1870s, usually in honour of such visiting foreign dignitaries as the Sultan of Turkey and the Shah of Persia. On the occasion of the Queen's Golden Jubilee in 1887, the town was en fête from the beginning of June until the end of July. The Jubilee itself was observed on 21 June when the troops of the garrison were reviewed on Southsea Common in the morning followed in the afternoon by festivities for 23,000 children. The town, as on previous gala occasions, was 'brilliantly illuminated'. The Naval Review by the Queen took place on 23 July. 136 ships took part and after dark they were each illuminated with coloured lights. It was rated an unqualified success and W.G. Gates was moved to hyperbole:

> The weather was perfect, the number of visitors unparalleled and the effect stupendous. It stirred the nation to its depths, as it was the greatest display of naval power that had ever been made in the history of the world.

Subsequent reviews took place in 1889 in honour of the Kaiser and in 1896 for a visit to Portsmouth by members of the House of Commons and for Li Hung Chang, the Chinese statesman, but they were minor affairs compared with the review which took place to mark the Diamond Jubilee of the Queen's succession in 1897, 'the like of which neither this nor any other port in the world had ever before witnessed', reported Gates. As well as

67   Review of the fleet at Spithead on 23 April 1856. It shows a mock gun-boat attack being carried out on Southsea Castle.

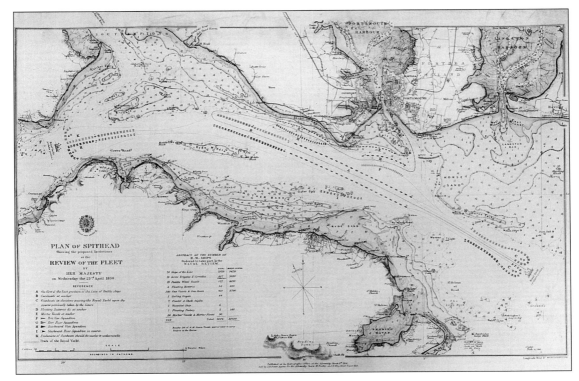

68 *Above.* A plan of Spithead showing the proposed evolutions at the fleet review, 23 April 1856.

69 *Left.* The Worcestershires on parade near Southsea Castle on 14 October 1800. Militia men like these helped rebuild the castle in 1813–14.

British ships, there was a huge assemblage of foreign warships. The British ships made up four lines, each five miles long, and were flanked in turn by another two columns, one of ships of foreign powers and the other of special merchant ships. The influx of visitors to Portsmouth and Gosport was unprecedented.

Reviews took place following the coronations of both King Edward VII in 1902 and King George V in 1911. By 1912 a more sober and sombre mood was prevailing. The review on 9 July 1912 for the members of both Houses of Parliament was for the legislators to see the strength of the Royal Navy. On this occasion, for the first time, aerial craft and hydroplanes were on display. Two years later, on 20 July 1914, the aim of the review was to test the efficiency of the Reserve system. It was, said Gates, 'a naval spectacle that outvied in power and majesty the many imposing fleet reviews that have from time to time taken place in those waters'. The king reviewed his ships off the Nab. Again, Gates was deeply moved. He described it as 'a spectacle unprecedented in naval history and, as each ship dipped its colours, one might well imagine the whispering wind

carrying the message, "those who are about to die salute you".' It was a sadly depleted fleet which the king inspected ten years later in July 1924.

On each of these occasions, Southsea Common and beach provided a splendid viewing platform not only for the local population but also for the many visitors drawn to the town by the promised spectacle. The spectacle was not confined to the sea. Southsea Castle and the Solent provided an equally impressive backdrop to events which took place on the Common itself. The garrison drilled there and troops were reviewed, presented with new colours or took part in mock battles on a regular basis to admiring audiences. Prince Albert presented new Colours to the 13th Light Infantry on 13 August 1846. Observers recorded that numbers of the nobility, yachtsmen 'and nearly all the distinguished families of the neighbourhood' including many strangers who had travelled long distances thronged Southsea and lined the roads to the Common to witness the ceremony 'which was one dense mass of well-dressed people'. A similar ceremony took place in 1879 when the Duchess of Connaught presented new colours to the

70 Presentation of Burmese Medals to the 80th Regiment (Staffordshire Volunteers) on Southsea Common, 30 June 1855.

71 The Portsmouth Volunteer Review, showing a detachment of troops marching on Southsea Castle on 8 May 1860.

72 The Portsmouth Volunteer Review performing a mock battle outside King William Gate on 8 May 1860.

1st Battalion 12th Regiment on Southsea Common, followed by a march past of all the troops in the Garrison and a Torchlight Tattoo.

Southsea Common was—and indeed still is—a piece of jealously guarded local open space. Occasionally someone or somebody interfered with what local people considered to be public rights of way or common land and there was a fierce reaction. Such an episode took place in 1874 when the Southsea Esplanade Pier Company, having obtained permission from both the War Office and the Admiralty, closed up the road between the corner of the Pier and the *Esplanade Hotel*, thus effectively preventing the local population taking a short cut along the beach and through the Sallyport into the old town from the Esplanade. The Pier Company was, basically, keen to preserve the exclusivity of its property. The Town Council was as outraged as its citizens and instructed the Town Clerk to prepare a removal notice but, before he could act, Mr. Barney Miller, a St Thomas's Ward councillor, with a gang of supporters

73 A review of troops on Southsea Common, *c*.1880.

74 The *Alert* and the *Discovery* leaving Portsmouth on an Arctic expedition, 5 June 1875.

75 The harbour and port defences come under an experimental naval attack in 1880.

broke down the Pier Company's barricade. It was promptly re-erected but taken down again the following night and burnt. For some days afterwards, unruly crowds gathered each evening in the vicinity of the pier and a certain amount of damage was done. On Saturday evening, 8 August, a crowd of some three or four thousand gathered round the pier. Stones were thrown and the mayor, fearing a major outbreak of violence, read the Riot Act and called in the military. Two companies of the 9th Regiment marched on the Common and began helping the police to clear the ground. Fighting broke out and it took several hours to restore order. Common sense prevailed and the Pier Company did not attempt to re-erect its barrier but the memory of these events lived on for a long time. Southsea society was outraged at the part played by local councillors in the insurrection. Others incurred a fair amount of opprobrium from different quarters too: the

police for unnecessary violence against the crowd, the magistrates for the harshness of the sentence they imposed on one of the perceived agitators and the pier directors for beginning the whole business in the first place. The Battle of Southsea, as the episode was described subsequently, is depicted in a painting which hung for many years in the *Barley Mow* public house, Castle Road. Today, the picture hangs in the City Museum and Records Office in Museum Road, a proud relic of a famous victory.

Southsea Castle itself had become increasingly dilapidated during the course of the 18th century. A major disaster took place in August 1759 when a huge explosion almost tore the building apart. Sparks from a fire in an upstairs room where food was being prepared are believed to have fallen through cracks in the floor boards and ignited loose powder in the room beneath where gunpowder and ball for muskets were stored belonging to the 72nd Regiment of Foot, camped then on the Common. Seventeen men, women and children were killed by the detonation. By the 1770s, the castle was described as ruinous.

Despite fear of invasion in 1797 and instructions to put the castle into a state of readiness, little was done to remedy its major structural deficiencies. It was not until 1812 when Major-General Benjamin Fisher became commanding officer of the Royal Engineers that serious work began on rebuilding Southsea Castle. Most of the work was done between 1813 and 1814 by a mixed workforce of soldiers and civilians. Fisher demolished the Tudor watch-tower and squared off the top of the keep, creating four positions for 24-pounder guns on the roof. The angled bastion facing the sea was reconstructed to create a much larger curved battery with magazines beneath, and a counterscarp gallery was built in the outer wall of the moat, linked to the castle by the caponier, a bomb-proof tunnel. The castle was strengthened further in the

mid-19th century as part of the general overhaul of the town's defences following the 1860 Royal Commission report. The report recognised the castle's importance defending the harbour's approaches and recommended the building of additional flanking batteries. Work on the east and west batteries began in 1863 and was completed by 1869. At the same time, the whole site was enclosed on the land side by a high brick wall with loopholes to enable the defenders to repel anyone attempting to overrun the complex from the north. These were the last major works to be carried out on the site before Portsmouth City Council purchased the now-redundant complex in 1960 and began the task of restoring the site to its 19th-century appearance.

Besides the activities of the navy and military, promenaders on Southsea seafront could also enjoy the yachting spectacle. Yachting initially was very much a sport for the wealthy. The 1890s saw some epic struggles between *Britannia* owned by the Prince of

76 Southsea Castle in the 1760s.

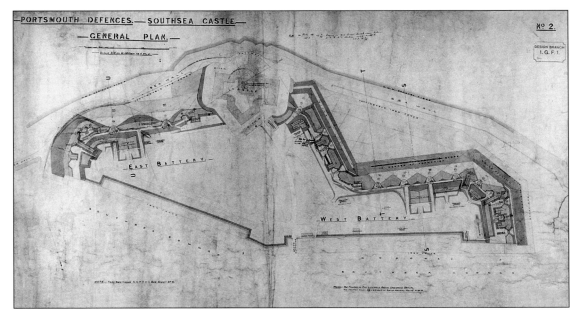

Wales and *Meteor*, the Kaiser's yacht, culminating in victory for *Britannia* in the Royal Albert Yacht Club Gold Challenge Cup in 1895 and victory the following year for the Kaiser and *Meteor*. The Royal Albert Yacht Club opened in 1865. The Royal Corinthian Yacht Club was founded in 1880 for amateurs at a time when small-yacht sailing and amateur seamanship had little or no patronage from the big clubs.

The Isle of Wight passenger ferries also contributed to the busy scene at sea. The first steam-packet service between Portsmouth and the Isle of Wight began in 1817. At that date— and for a few more years yet—there were also regular sailings twice a week from the *Quebec Tavern* in Bath Square, Point to Le Havre, daily sailings to Cowes from the *King's Head*, Point as well as the twice daily sailings to Ryde. Packets also left three times a week from the *Thatched House,* Point for Lymington and from the *White Hart* for Southampton. Other vessels plied between Point and the West Country and once a week there was a service to Guernsey from the *True Blue* on Point. The advent of the railway put paid to much of this coastal shipping with the exception, of course, of

77 A plan of Southsea Castle in 1893 which shows the building works of the 1860s.

78 The king's yacht, *Britannia,* leading off Southsea, after 1901.

services to the Isle of Wight which grew in popularity as a holiday destination during Victoria's reign. When trains first arrived at the Town Station in 1847, passengers for the Isle of Wight had to take a horse-drawn cab or horse bus from the station to the Common Hard in Portsea for their connecting ferry. When the Clarence Pier opened in 1861 the ferry companies—the Southsea and Isle of Wight Steam Ferry Company and the Isle of White Steam Packet Company—transferred to this new facility, built to handle two paddle steamers simultaneously. The whole business of moving passengers from the Town Station to their ferry connection was speeded up dramatically in 1865 when the Landport and Southsea Tramway inaugurated its service between the Town Station and Clarence Pier. The tramway terminus was actually inside the Town Station and horses pulled the cars and luggage vans along rails which ran down the Terraces, along Pier Road and onto the very pier itself. The opening of the Harbour Station in 1876 changed things yet again. Passengers

walked the few yards from their trains to the new landing stage at the end of the Harbour Station. In 1880 the railways bought out the ferry companies and created an integrated service which by the 1920s was carrying two million passengers a year between Portsmouth and Ryde.

Sea bathing had been enjoyed since the mid-18th century when the bathing house, Quebec House, was built by public subscription in Bath Square. Bathing machines were available for hire on the beach from the late 18th century and hot baths were to be had, too, in a wooden building near the Little Morass, a predecessor of the more substantial edifice built after 1816. William White described the beach in front of the Clarence Esplanade in 1859 as well adapted for sea bathing 'and the numerous bathing machines ranged along it ... as convenient as those of any other bathing place on the coast'.

These were facilities, however, for the wealthier sections of local society. The less well-off, the men that is, did not worry about such

Royal Albert Yacht Club.

PATRON—HIS MAJESTY THE KING.

Commodore—T. M. LORD, Esq.   Vice Commodore—M. B. KENNEDY, Esq.
" WINIFRED," 186 Tons.   " WHITE HEATHER," 179 Tons.
Rear-Commodore—H. J. MASON, Esq.
" EVONA," 534 Tons.

SOLENT CLASS REGATTAS, 1910.

Races will take place as under:—
FRIDAY, JUNE 17th, FRIDAY, JULY 8th, and FRIDAY, JULY 22nd.

CLASS.		ENTRANCE FEES; NON-MEMBERS.			PRIZES;		
					1st	2nd	3rd
YACHTS OF 10 METRE CLASS		12/-	...	...	£6	£3	£1
do.	9 do.	10/-	...	...	£5	£2	£1
do.	8 do.	8/-	...	...	£4	£2	£1
do.	7 do.	6/-	...	...	£3	30/	15/-
do.	6 do.	6/-	...	...	£3	30/-	15/-
do.	5 do.	4/-	...	...	£2	£1	10/-

THE ANNUAL REGATTA

Will take place on FRIDAY, 12th AUGUST, 1910.
All Matches open to Yachts belonging to any Royal or Recognised
YACHT CLUB, ENGLISH or FOREIGN.
ELEVEN RACES forming the Programme, the two most important
being:
RACE FOR YACHTS OF THE 23 METRE CLASS.
1st Prize, The "Albert Cup." 2nd Prize, £25.
ENTRANCE FEES:—Members, £2 10s.; Non-Members, £5.
RACE FOR YACHTS OF THE 15 METRE CLASS.
1st Prize, CUP.; 2nd Prize, £20; 3rd Prize, £10; 4th Prize, £5.
ENTRANCE FEES:—Members, 30/-. Non-Members, £3.

Royal Portsmouth Corinthian Yacht Club.

Commodore—THE RT. HON. THE EARL OF DUDLEY.
Vice-Commodore—H. MARZETTI, Esq.
Hon. Secretary—MAJOR MIALL, Club House, Southsea.

YACHTING PROGRAMME FOR 1910.

Races will take place as under:—

SATURDAY, JUNE 11th, SATURDAY, JUNE 25th, SATURDAY,
JULY 16th, and AUGUST 13th.
To comprise the undermentioned Races on each occasion. 1st Race,
12 noon. Ten minutes interval.

CLASS:		ENTRANCE FEES; MEMBERS.	NON-MEMBERS.		PRIZES;		
					1st	2nd	3rd
CRUISER HANDICAP	...	5/-	10/-	...	£6	£3	30/-
10 METRE CLASS	...	5/-	10/-	...	£6	£3	30/-
8	do.	4/-	8/-	...	£6	£3	30/-
7	do.	3/6	6/6	...	£5	50/-	20/-
6	do.	3/-	6/-	...	£3	30/-	15/-
REDWINGS	...	1/-	2/-	...	£3	10/-	5/-
MERMAIDS	...	1/-	2/-	...	£2	20/-	10/-

ALL ENTRIES CLOSE 2 DAYS previous to the RACES respectively, excepting
REDWINGS and MERMAIDS which are POST ENTRIES.

paraphernalia as bathing machines, attendants and bathing costumes. They just stripped off in warm weather and, leaving their clothes on the beach, plunged in. There were few objections to the unclothed bathing off the more remote stretches of the beach beyond Southsea Castle but the sight of nude male bathers near Clarence Pier and the King's Rooms was a regular source of complaint from the 1830s.

Swimming was clearly a popular local pastime. The Portsmouth Swimming Club was established in 1875 and by the end of the century had nearly 1,500 'contributing' members including about 600 ladies. The headquarters during the summer months was Southsea beach. The Corporation baths in Landport were used during the winter. Visitors were permitted to join the club and use its swimming instruction stages on Southsea beach for a small charge. Annual races were held in the open sea during July, for the senior and junior championship and, also, a race for the lady champion of the club.

79 *Above left.* Yachting off Southsea between the Wars.

80 *Above.* Advertisements for the Royal Albert Yacht Club and the Royal Portsmouth Corinthian Yacht Club in the 1910 *Official Guide.*

81   Trams at Clarence Pier in 1910.

There used also to be an annual regatta, held in the harbour during July or August 'for the amusement of the inhabitants and visitors, and the encouragement of skill and energy among the watermen'. The ferry boat men competed for prizes mainly in the harbour but the larger boats raced out to Spithead and back. The Queen and the Prince Consort honoured the regatta with their presence on the Royal Yacht, the *Fairy*, on 11-12 July 1849. The weather was superb, it was reported, and the sport excellent. There were still some 300 ferry boats in 1859 employed in conveying passengers between Gosport, Portsmouth, Portsea and other places within the harbour as well as to and from Spithead, and the regatta was a keenly anticipated event. A small ferry with a handful of passengers on board, doubtless bound for Spithead, is captured in choppy seas by Turner in his watercolour of a scene off the entrance of Portsmouth Harbour in *Gosport, the Entrance to Portsmouth Harbour, c.*1829, purchased in 1997 by Portsmouth City Council. The Southsea Rowing Club was founded in 1860 by enthusiastic local amateurs. The club has survived to the present-day and its boat house and club house still stand on the Clarence Esplanade.

82 Bathing machines, *c*.1805.

83 Bathing stages belonging to the Portsmouth Swimming Club seen here in 1908.

84 J.M.W. Turner's 'Gosport. The Entrance to Portsmouth Harbour', *c*.1829.

Chapter Six

Cleanliness

Despite many advantages, natural and otherwise, the new resort and residential suburb of Southsea was not immune to the cholera outbreak of 1848-9 which began in Fountain Street, Landport and spread rapidly through the poorest streets of that district and into neighbouring middle-class districts. The subsequent report to the General Board of Health on the sewerage, drainage and water supply of Portsmouth, carried out in 1850 by Robert Rawlinson, Civil Engineer, and the General Board of Health's Superintending Inspector, in response to a petition to the Board from a group of local ratepayers, provides a useful overview of the physical condition of the borough in the mid-19th century.

The description of conditions in the old town of Portsmouth—the lack of a decent water-supply, inadequate lighting, cleansing, watching and regulating and the appalling state of the parish churchyard—makes it all too painfully clear why those who were able to do so quit the old town once there was suitable alternative accommodation. However, the newly-constructed Terraces still abutted on to the houses of Croxton Town. Steel Street, Southsea was described by Mr. Piercey, Surgeon of the Portsmouth Town District and of part of Southsea, as 'a narrow, ill-ventilated street, composed of small, ill-built tenements'. Concluding this evidence he remarked:

> The whole of the houses in my Southsea district, especially as connected with the habitations of the poor, are badly built, the streets

and courts are undrained, the water-supply is deficient, and the inhabitants are continually subject to epidemics.

The situation had not improved one jot in the five years since a previous inspection of these streets by Mr. J.R. Martin in 1845 had noted:

> Wherever the working classes are massed, there we are sure to find all the conditions unfavourable to health ... The dwellings of the labouring population are described as defective in construction; many houses are erected back to back, and the ground floors of all are excessively damp; the streets are long, narrow, dilapidated, damp, and filthy beyond description. Dr Quarrier observed of them, that in Gold-Street new sovereigns would be tarnished; in Silver-Street, silver would rapidly assume the colour of pewter or lead; in Steel-Street, steel would be rusted by the noxious vapours arising from accumulations of all kinds of filth and deleterious gases.

Evidence was also given 'as to the want of proper Sanitary Works even to the best Class of Property'. Mr. S.P. Pritchard of 'South-end', Green Lane wrote to inform the inquiry of a sink at the end of Green Lane, Somers Town, near Trafalgar Cottage and his premises, which was constructed while he was at sea and therefore unable to object. The smell in warm weather was offensive in the extreme and his late neighbour, Commander Franklin, lost a son 'some time back' and, only a few weeks since, a daughter 'from fever'. In addition, he drew the Inquiry's attention to the turning from

Somers Street to Green Lane which 'is always strewed with vegetable litter, ashes, and rubbish thrown out from the houses; the road is generally muddy and in bad condition'. Another resident, Mr. John Turnbull of 6, River Street, Green Lane, also wrote, listing the nuisances with which he and his family had to contend:

> ... owing to the want of a gutter or water-course, and there being no drainage in the vicinity of the above-named place, the smell at all times is intolerable.

He pointed out, like Mr. Pritchard, that much could be done to improve the area if his neighbours could be prevailed upon to be more cleanly but, whenever he had tried to reason with them about throwing rubbish out onto the streets 'such as suds, decayed vegetables, ashes, &c.', he had met with nothing but abuse. He also highlighted another form of nuisance in the developing suburb:

> an excavation dug out near my dwelling for the purpose of building; it is left without any railing or fence round it, close to the public thoroughfare. One young man some time ago died through the injuries sustained by falling into the place so dug out.

Dr. Raper of Landport had more to say about the areas under development:

> In the vicinity of streets that are now building, or recently built, it is not very uncommon to have large pools of green and foetid water standing for weeks and months together, and infecting the atmosphere all around: of this examples may be seen in the neighbourhood of Grosvenor-street.

The incidence of disease testified to the prevailing insanitary conditions across the borough. Between 1841 and 1847, the annual rate of mortality to the thousand in Portsmouth was 25-37, independent of the much greater mortality recorded in 1848 and, again, in 1849 from cholera. A fair standard then was reckoned to be 15 per thousand.

The present state and condition of the borough was 'fearful' in Robert Rawlinson's words. He further quoted the medical officer to the City of London who wrote in 1849:

> the frightful phenomenon of a periodic pestilence belongs only to defective sanitary arrangements; and in comparing one local death-rate with another, it is requisite to remember that, in addition to the ordinary redundance of deaths which marks an unhealthy district, there is a tendency from time to time to the recurrence of epidemic pestilence, which visits all unhealthy districts disproportionately, and renders their annual excess of mortality still more egregious and glaring.

The cholera outbreak of 1848-9 was undoubtedly just such an epidemic pestilence. What was to be done? 'Unity of Action in the Borough' was what was proposed by Rawlinson and many of his key witnesses, including Thomas Ellis Owen, who was actually mayor in 1848 when the major outbreak of cholera began. He spoke at the inquiry at some length, as 'a civil engineer and surveyor'. He referred to the map he had compiled in 1838 for the Tithe Commissioners and another compiled a few years previously when Landport and Southsea had applied to Parliament for an Act to pave, drain and light those districts. Through knowledge acquired during those mapping exercises, he was, he said, well-informed as regards drainage issues on Portsea Island. The crying evil, he said, was that all refuse-drainage had to pass over the surface. The fall of these surface-gutters was small and the movement of the water therefore sluggish. Consequently, during the summer months the stench from these gutters was intolerable. The construction of underground drains was the answer. He also said:

> I ... think it of extreme importance that the towns of Portsmouth and Portsea, together with the towns of Landport and Southsea, should be included under one system of management, and that the powers of the existing Acts should be incorporated into one under the 'Public Health Act', and placed under the general management of the Town

Council. My reasons for this recommendation are that one set of officers, from having more duties to perform, and being better paid, would be more efficient, and because considerable inconvenience is at present experienced from different laws applying to different parts of the borough ...

What Thomas Ellis Owen was referring to was the fact that the administration of the borough was divided between the newly-reformed Borough Council, elected by ratepayers with authority to legislate by bye-law and appoint town clerks and treasurers, and with administrative powers over police, finance and property, and the *ad hoc* bodies established by private acts of Parliament in the late 18th century to grapple with the problems of drainage, paving, street lighting and cleansing, which arose as Portsmouth first began to spread beyond the walls of the old town. The unreformed corporation was not empowered to embrace these issues. Ironically, in their turn, the Improvement Commissioners for Portsmouth and Portsea, despite obtaining additional powers by further acts of Parliament in the 1840s—to acquire lands for purposes of street widening, for prevention of nuisances, for lighting, for regulation of hackney coaches and porters, and to enable then to levy additional rates for improvements—had still failed to get to grips with these issues. Robert Rawlinson easily dismissed their efforts to talk up their achievements:

There is sufficient reply to ... these statements ... that the paving is sufficient and good, the cleansing regular, 'three times a week', that the lighting is all which can be desired, and the water-supply most unexceptionable. The returns of the medical officers state the direct contrary, and there is other evidence to show that the lighting is most imperfect, and the water-supply deficient, costly and bad in quality.

To sum up, Rawlinson found that the borough was not as healthy as it might be on account of its ill-paved and uncleansed streets, imperfect privy accommodation, crowded

courts and houses with large, exposed middens and cesspools nearby—and no adequate power for effective local government. Disease was distinctly traceable to ill-drained and crowded districts of the borough, to inadequate ventilation, to the absence of a clean water-supply and of sewers and drains. He recommended that a system of street, courtyard and house drainage was put in place, that a constant and cheap supply of pure water, under pressure, was laid to every house and yard to supersede all local wells and pumps, that water-closets or soilpan apparatus be substituted for the noxious privies and cesspools, and that regular and systematic removal of all refuse should take place at short intervals. Courts and passages should also be properly paved and there should be a regular system of washing and cleansing all courts, passages, slaughterhouses, footpaths, and surface channels in the borough, and that all roads should be properly maintained. All these advantages could be secured under the Public Health Act and he urged its early adoption.

The Council acted at once and in a memorial to the Government referred to the expediency of investing in them sufficient powers to implement the Public Health Act. Battle was now joined with the Improvement Commissioners—and would last, incredibly, for some years. The Commissioners were determined not to give up without a fight. They managed to engineer enough opposition amongst the wealthier sections of the local population—alarmed by the likely costs of implementing the Public Health Act—to force the Council to rescind its resolution to adopt the Act. There was a further abortive attempt by the Council to secure the adoption of the Act in 1853 and, although the decision was taken to proceed—by a majority of one, it was postponed shortly afterwards. The Commissioners were invincible and in fact in 1857 a further Improvement Act was obtained, the Landport and Southsea Improvement Act, which created a new set of 36 commissioners for dealing with those parts of the borough not included in the Portsea Improvement Act of 1843 and the Portsmouth Improvement Act of 1848. The powers annexed to the new act were considerable. No house thereafter was to be erected in these districts without a drainage system, roads and streets were to be paved and flagged, and courts and passages flagged and drained. Land could be purchased for street widening, markers provided and slaughterhouses erected. Rating powers were also granted. However, obtaining an act was one thing; implementing it, quite another and it was the lamentable mismanagement of the Landport and Southsea Board which provided the catalyst for change at long last. On 14 April 1863 a great meeting of Southsea residents took place at the *Portland Hall*, the assembly rooms built by Thomas Ellis Owen next to the *Portland Hotel*, to protest against the inefficiency of the Board of Commissioners. There was a great deal of plain speaking and calls for better government of this growing district including demands for secession from the rest of the town. The Town Council was galvanised into action and on 31 May 1863 voted by 46 to 8 to adopt the Local Government Act of 1858 which empowered them to abolish the Commissioners and take over their duties as the Local Board of Health. The council met as the Local Board of Health for the first time on 3 August 1864. A clerk and treasurer were appointed, a Drainage and Sewerage Committee and a Roads and Works Committee whose duties would include the paving, lighting, cleansing, watering and management of the streets and roads. A Finance Committee was also appointed and a General Purposes Committee for licensing and regulating hackney carriages and carrying out such other tasks as might be assigned it. The newly-appointed committees set to work with enthusiasm. The Drainage and Sewerage Committee reported back the following month with a scheme for the effective draining of the borough devised by the newly-appointed Borough Engineer,

Mr. Lewis Angell, the estimated cost being £90,000. The scheme was adopted and construction began in 1865. The borough was split into a high- and low-level drainage area. Drainage from the higher levels of Portsea, Landport and Upper Southsea was intercepted and carried direct to the outfall at the entrance to Langstone Harbour, quite independently of the low-level system to the south. The scheme was essentially gravitational but was supplemented by lifting power provided by the pumping station built in Henderson Road in 1868. Mains drainage was the major single contributing factor in the reduction in due course of the death-rate in the community from 25.3 to 10.76 per thousand.

Mains drainage and sewerage issues were clearly dealt with quickly and effectively and to the general satisfaction of Southsea's residents. Roads and works matters, however, were less easily resolved. On 17 December 1877 a meeting was called by a group of influential residents at the Portland Hall to consider a number of clearly vexatious—and familiar—issues, most importantly 'the very bad and neglected condition of the Roads, Footpaths, Drainage and Lighting of Southsea and especially, East Southsea'. The meeting would also consider sending a memorial to the Local Government Board in London asking the Board to despatch an Inspector to inquire into the causes of their complaints and 'the absence of care, control and watchfulness' of the local authority over the inhabitants of 'this large and important WATERING PLACE and Sea-side resort of SOUTHSEA'. If nothing was done to improve the present situation, the meeting would also consider separating from the borough of Portsmouth and constituting itself a new town with its own urban sanitary authority calling itself the Town of Southsea. Almost 250 local residents supported the calling of the meeting, styling themselves 'owners and occupiers of important residential property at Southsea' and indeed most of them lived in the heart of Thomas Ellis Owen's Southsea

THE OADS AND FOOTPATHS OF SOUTHSEA.

We the undersigned, beg to call a PUBLIC MEETING of Residents in Southsea, and others interested in its prosperity, to be held at the PORTLAND HALL, on MONDAY NEXT, the 17th December, at 3 p m., when the Chair will be taken by Major General R. N. WESTROPP, for the purpose of taking into consideration the following matters :—

1st.—The very bad and neglected condition of the Roads, Footpaths, Drainage, and Lighting of Southsea, and more especially that portion of it called East Southsea.

2nd.—The periodical Inundations in the Winter which cause many of the Roads to be frequently impassable and render Houses in their immediate vicinity in many cases uninhabitable.

3rd.—To Memorialise the Local Government Board in London to send down an Inspector to inquire into the causes which lead to this condition of things, and to the absence of care, control, and watchfulness on the part of the Local Board of the Borough of Portsmouth, over the health and comfort and general convenience of the Inhabitants of this large and important WATERING PLACE and Sea-side resort of SOUTHSEA.

4th.—To advise with the Government Inspector as to the apparent inability of the Borough Authorities to exercise and put in force their Legal Powers, by which the Roads and Footpaths may all be formed and made up, and the Owners of Property (where liable) be compelled to bear the Cost ; and if a satisfactory assurance cannot be given that immediate improvement will commence, then to advise with the Government Inspector as to the desirability of obtaining an Act or Parliament by which the whole of the District of Southsea extending as far as Langstone Harbour to the East, may be separated from the Borough of Portsmouth, constituted a NEW TOWN, placed under its own governing URBAN SANITARY AUTHORITY, and called the TOWN OF SOUTHSEA.

R. M. Westropp, Major-General, Rosenheim Villa
T. W. Playfair, Major-Gen., R.E., Cumberland House
Edwin Galt, Lieut.-Col , J P. for Portsmouth, Beach Mansions
F. Wood, Eastern Parade
J. Lush, Queen's Crescent
Charles James Mew, Palmerston Road, Southsea
T. Fleming, Waverly House, Southsea
Thos. W. Earwaker, Waverley Grove, Southsea
W. Oddie, Wytham Lodge
William B. Baird, St. Simon's Road
Charles Lanyon Owen, Lieut.-Col., J P. for Portsmouth, 4, Portland Terrace
L. Poynder, Lennox Cottage, Clarendon Road
F. Baldey, St. Simon's Vicarage, Waverley Road
Eustace Neville Rolfe, J P., Co. Norfolk, 4, Eastern Parade, and Sedgeford Hall, King's Lynn
T. Q. Meade, Major, R M A., Clydagh Lodge, Eastern Parade
J. N. Heard, M A., 13, Eastern Parade
Henry Fyffe, M A., Clerk in Holy Orders, St. Helen's College, South Parade and Burgoyne Road
J. Griffin, J P. 2, Eastern Parade
Joseph Blake, Vicar of St. Jude's
Henry Chads, Admiral
A. Slocock, 7, Clarence Parade
Frederick Warren, Capt., R.N., Palmyra Villa
Arthur H. Byng, Rugby House
Edmund Heathcote, Vice-Admiral, Frogmore House
J. G. Bickford, Rear-Admiral, 1, Hope Villa
W. H. Axford, Warwick House
C. H. Binstead, South Beach House
W. H. Perfect, LL.B , Barrister
S. Pittis, Granada Road
W. Cairns Armstrong, Stepney Towers
A. Montgomery, Capt., Lorraine Villa
Arthur Batcher, Major-General, Granada Road
W. H. Douglas, Perth House
And 201 other owners and occupiers of important residential property at Southsea.

All Residents in Southsea are earnestly requested to attend

THE STATE OF THE ROADS AT SOUTHSEA.
PUBLIC MEETING OF THE INHABITANTS.

On Monday afternoon a public meeting was held at the Portland Hall for the purpose of taking into consideration the following matters :—

1st.—The very bad and neglected condition of the roads, footpaths, drainage, and lighting of Southsea, and more especially that portion of it called East Southsea.

2nd.—The periodical inundations in the winter which cause many of the roads to be frequently impassable and render houses in their immediate vicinity in many cases uninhabitable.

3rd.—To memorialise the Local Government Board in London to send down an Inspector to inquire into the causes which lead to this condition of things, and to the absence of care, control, and watchfulness on the part of the Local Board of the borough of Portsmouth, over the health and comfort and general convenience of the inhabitants of this large and important watering-place and sea-side resort of Southsea.

4th.—To advise with the Government Inspector as to the apparent inability of the Borough Authorities to exercise and put in force their legal powers, by which the roads and footpaths may all be formed and made up, and the owners of property (where liable) be compelled to bear the cost, and if a satisfactory assurance cannot be given that immediate improvement will commence, then to advise with the Government Inspector as to the desirability of obtaining an Act of Parliament by which the whole of the district of Southsea, extending as far as Langstone Harbour to the east, may be separated from the borough of Portsmouth, constituted a new town, placed under its own governing Urban Sanitary Authority, and called the Town of Southsea.

In the absence of Major-General Westropp, Colonel Charles Lanyon Owen presided, and there was a large and influential attendance, including the Rev. H. Fyffe, M.A., Rev. W. H. Williamson, Colonel F. I. Conway Gordon, J.P., General Mould, R.E., General Playfair, Dr. Jolliffe, Dr. Lloyd Owen, Colonel Galt, J.P., Colonel Urmston, Captain Raby, V.C. Dr. Smith, Dr. Axford, Dr. Cousins, Mr. Alderman Chambers, J.P., Mr. Alderman Batchelor, Messrs. Joseph Lush, A. F. Perkins, G. E. Kent, Houghton, Wainscott, J. T. Helby, E. K. Stace, T. Caine, Larcome, W. Oddie, Barnes, T. Fleming, G. White, D. Whitehall, E. G. Holbrook, A. Ford, C. J. Mew, C. J. Walker, W. Carrell, &c.

85 & 86 Cuttings from the *Hampshire Telegraph* relating to the roads and footpaths of Southsea, 1877.

development. Chief amongst this core of residents was Lieutenant Colonel Charles Lanyon Owen of 4, Portland Terrace, who spoke of the Owen family's interests in these issues at the meeting itself. He had calculated that he and his relations owned property in Southsea worth £80,000.

Colonel Owen chaired the meeting at the Portland Hall where, one after another, local residents rose to voice their complaints about 'the periodical inundations at Southsea'. Put briefly, surface guttering and related drainage was not adequate to take away the water after heavy rainfall and few of even the busiest thoroughfares had decent road surfaces, let alone raised walkways at the sides of the roads. Osborne, Kent and Marmion Roads all came in for criticism as did South Parade and Clarence Parade. Wits in the audience cited the lady who lived in Portland Road who had been away for two years, and told the speaker that 'on her return ... she saw the same puddle in it as before she went away'. Another speaker

87 South Parade showing the parlous state of the road surface.

88 Clarence Parade, again showing the dry, dusty state of the road.

89   King's Road showing a well-made side pavement but a poor road surface.

told of holes in the road near the Common where 'from September to October they might have captured a large basket of eels ... , and from October to now a lot of minnows'. Colonel Galt of Beach Mansions spoke for many in the audience when he said that although the Local Government Act had been introduced in 1864, he failed to see that anything had been done by the authorities for the improvement of the roads being discussed 'and the amelioration of the general condition of the place'. He also raised the spectre of the aggrieved visitor who compared Southsea very unfavourably with Folkestone, Brighton, Worthing, Eastbourne, Hastings and Bournemouth. He continued:

> They considered themselves a highly civilised and progressive watering-place, they offered inducements for visitors, advertised the place,

and built large blocks of houses for visitors, and the result was that nothing was done for them which ought to be done.

Others, with long memories, expressed fears of disease from the accumulations of mud and refuse in the streets in their neighbourhoods. There was Victoria Road with water and mud an inch or two deep and Exmouth Road and Albert Road where what drainage there was overflowed after heavy rain and 'all kinds of filth and abominations' erupted into the street. Mr. Joseph Lush complained:

> For the last 15 years he had resided in Queens-crescent and for 15 dreary winters what had been his prospect? Mud and dirt, and slush of all descriptions, supplemented occasionally by broken bottles, bricks and scrapings of tin, which some sympathetic costermonger had deposited for the good of his neighbours.

Dr. Axford of Warwick House reserved his condemnation for Merton Road:

> ... it was in a notoriously bad condition, full of holes in some places and in others a perfect pond. Those who drove through the road in carriages were put to great inconvenience and annoyance, for their wheels were no sooner out of one hole than they were into another. The road was highly dangerous.

The meeting resolved to set up the Southsea Improvement Association 'for the purpose of watching over and protecting the interests of Southsea, in order that it may keep pace with other South Coast watering places'. Major-General Westropp was appointed President, and Colonels Lanyon Owen and Galt, Mr. Lush and Mr. Albert Besant, Vice-Presidents. The Association set to work at once, preparing the memorial to be sent to the Local Government Board and collecting information 'relative to the neglected and dangerous state of the roads &c.'.

A deputation led by Major-General Westropp and his Vice-Presidents and accompanied by local MP, Sir James Elphinstone, waited upon the President of the Local Government Board in London only a month later, reported the *Southsea Observer* on 18 January 1878. An official inquiry was ordered and opened on 16 March. The Inspector concurred with the members of the Southsea Improvement Association. The Corporation had duties and powers with regard to roads and streets and there was no excuse for the non-repair of so-called private roads. The Corporation had attempted to argue at the inquiry that their powers were limited where 'private' roads were concerned. At the end of the inquiry, the Corporation surrendered, so to speak, and gave an undertaking 'that immediate improvement will commence'.

The Association agreed to stay its hand and wait 'for the fulfilment of the promise ... that the work of repairing and making up the roads and footpaths of Southsea should proceed immediately and with all due diligence'. They agreed, however, not to wind up the Association quite yet, to maintain a watching brief on progress and to 'invite their members to report to them, at their meetings which will be held from time to time, the names of streets, roads and footpaths still requiring repair'.

Progress was clearly not quick enough for another—furious—memorial was despatched within twelve months to the Local Government Board asking for a separate sanitary authority for Southsea. 'Your memorialists', the Association wrote:

> fail to see that the slightest effort has been made by the Portsmouth Urban Sanitary Authority towards the developing of the manifold attractions of Southsea. The greater part of New Southsea remains in the same unfinished and dilapidated state that it has remained in for years, with bad roads and no footpaths ...

Whether the necessary works were in hand already or this latest salvo galvanised the local authority into action, it is now impossible to say. Certainly, no separate urban sanitary authority ever materialised and, at a meeting of the Southsea Improvement Association at the *Beach Mansions Hotel* on 12 July 1879, it was proposed and carried unanimously that:

> the thanks of the Association be tendered to the Mayor and Town Council of the Borough for having taken in hand the Repairs and making-up of a large number of the Roads and Footpaths of Southsea.

Satisfaction had been obtained at long last and the Association could turn its attention now to further improvements.

Chapter Seven

Godliness

Since the mid–16th century, special forms of prayer and special services, meditation and public fasting had been recommended for use by healthy congregations in areas

FORM

OF

PRAYER AND THANKSGIVING

TO

ALMIGHTY GOD,

TO BE USED

In all Churches and Chapels in England and Wales, on THURSDAY, the 15th day of November, being the Day appointed for a GENERAL THANKSGIVING to Almighty God:

To acknowledge His great Goodness and Mercy in removing from us that grievous Disease with which many Parts of this Kingdom have been lately visited.

LEGG, PORTSMOUTH.

90 The title page of the Form of Prayer and Thanksgiving service held for the disappearance of the cholera, 15 November 1849.

stricken by the plague and other infections. A day of humiliation and prayer for relief from the scourge of cholera was designated in Portsmouth on 26 September 1849. The dockyard and other government establishments were closed and local shops and businesses suspended activities for the day. Special prayers for relief from the epidemic were offered in all the local churches and chapels. Whether or not it was divine intervention or the cooler weather, the epidemic had run its course by mid-November and on 15 November general thanksgiving services across the town celebrated the disappearance of the cholera. Notices of the services which took place at the old parish church of St Thomas's still survive in a volume of ephemera entitled 'Records of Portsmouth Parish Church' compiled by local antiquarians W.H. Saunders and Alfred Everitt in the early 20th century. At the height of the cholera outbreak, victims were being buried in St Thomas's churchyard in batches, usually before 8 a.m.

Southsea was in fact in the ancient parish of St Mary's Portsea, although its earliest residents were a great deal nearer Portsmouth parish church and without doubt would have worshipped there if they were Anglicans until Southsea's first church, St Paul's, was built, chiefly by parliamentary grant, and opened in 1823 with 1,600 sittings, 900 of which were free. The vicar of Portsmouth at the time, Charles Brune Henville, in fact not only made a handsome contribution to the costs of building

91 Notice of services to be held on account of the re-appearance of cholera, 14 October 1853.

PARISH OF PORTSMOUTH.

SPECIAL SERVICES

On account of the re-appearance of Cholera in England.

UNDER THE SANCTION OF THE LORD BISHOP OF WINCHESTER,

Special Services,

In order to beseech Almighty God to avert the pestilence from this Neighbourhood, and to withdraw it altogether, will be held in the CHURCHES of

ST. THOMAS & ST. MARY,

IN THIS PARISH,

On FRIDAY, Oct. 14th, 1853,

At Half-past Eight o'Clock in the Morning, and at a Quarter before Seven in the Evening.

92 St Thomas's Church c.1910.

93 The north-west view of St Paul's Church, *c*.1823.

the church but also made it a gift of a silver communion service. St Paul's was situated in the square to which it gave its name at the junction of King Street and Landport Street, behind Hampshire and Landport Terraces. It was allotted an ecclesiastical district in 1835.

Southsea's social mix was well demonstrated here, in St Paul's Square, where, on the south side, large stuccoed, terraced houses were occupied by the middle classes and on the north side were small, artisan dwellings. The church was built on land given by Daniel and Henry Hewitt and designed by Francis Goodwin. It cost some £16,000, £14,000 of which came from the parliamentary grant and the rest from voluntary subscriptions. The building, in Perpendicular style, was clad in Bath stone and, with its array of pinnacles including the four 'highly ornamental' turrets at each corner, over 80 feet high, is easily distinguished in early prints and drawings and, later, photographs of Southsea. It had one of the largest, single-span roofs in the country when it was built, the single-cell interior having no supporting pillars. It did not have a sanctuary nor a chancel, the altar being set simply against the east wall beneath the cast-iron rose window. Cast iron

was used elsewhere, on other window frames and the small pillars of the galleries. St Paul's was a perpetual curacy and the patronage lay in the gift of the vicar of Portsea. The church was destroyed in the 1939-45 war in the first blitz, on the night of 10-11 January 1941, and former members of the congregation remember vividly the flames leaping through the great rose window.

St Paul's remained Southsea's only church for some years. Admittedly, St James' Milton was built, by voluntary subscription and public grants, and opened in 1841, but Milton was still a rural hamlet of farms, labourers' cottages and fishermen's dwellings on the other side of Portsea Island. Its new church had no impact on Southsea and its needs. It was another 10 years before the next church, St Jude's Church, opened—twenty years after St Paul's opened its doors for the first time.

The diocesan authorities in Winchester (Portsmouth did not become a separate diocese until 1927) were well aware of the problems—the lack of sufficient sittings and proper pastoral care in Portsmouth's or, to be more accurate, the parish of Portsea's, growing suburbs—but they were faced with the total intransigence of the vicar of St Mary's Portsea, J.V. Stewart, who had taken up his position in 1838. His opposition to change of any sort which might affect his income severely hampered progress on church extension in Southsea for almost half a century. He died in office in 1878 aged 85. The creation of a new parish required the consent of those affected by the proposed changes and his consent would not be given easily.

The Archdeacon of Winchester, Joseph Wigram, was not prepared to tolerate this state of affairs. He set about collecting a formidable amount of information on the spiritual condition of Portsea which lay in his archdeaconry in order more effectively to make his case for reform. Outside the walled town of Portsea, there were three Anglican churches where the residents of Southsea might go: St Mary's Portsea, the church of the ancient parish, All Saints, Landport and St Paul's. The Archdeacon's facts speak for themselves. St Mary's had a local resident population of 5,000 persons. The church could accommodate 1,300 but only a very small proportion of those sittings were free. All Saints, Landport, like St Paul's built by parliamentary grant but opened five years later in 1828, had a population of 13,000 and 1,600 sittings of which 1,100 were free. It had only 130 communicants. St Paul's had a population of 16,000 and, of its 1,600 sittings, 900 were free. There were only 100 communicants. Put bluntly, there were only 4,500 sittings available for a population probably in excess of 34,000 by the late 1840s and, of those 4,500 sittings, only 2,000 were free. The Archdeacon did not mince his words which Nigel Yates quotes in his *Portsmouth Paper,* 'The Anglican Revival in Victorian Portsmouth':

> The working classes and the poor superabound, and under circumstances unhappily calculated to produce the greatest moral evils. The want of due pastoral influence and restraint among them is appalling. The ordinary vices connected with garrison and seaport towns grievously prevail ...

> That amidst such a state of things, multitudes of children should remain unbaptised, that the worship of God should be disregarded by thousands of adults, that ordinances should be despised—who can be surprised? They are without Christ and without hope.

The Archdeacon was particularly depressed by the fact that accommodation in the local beer shops and public houses outnumbered church sittings by approximately two to one.

The church had to fight back and to do this he proposed, late in 1849, to build four new churches, three in Landport and one in Southsea. He had found a benefactor for the Southsea church already in Thomas Ellis Owen. The Archdeacon also proposed building eight new parsonage houses and five new church schools. He also devised a package of measures for the more effective administration and management of the parishes of St George's and St John's within the town of Portsea but J.V. Stewart would have none of this despite strong support for the proposal at a public meeting. The wrangling became so protracted that Thomas Ellis Owen decided to go ahead with his church in Southsea on his own. If need be, it would function as a proprietary chapel. St Jude's, opposite Portland Terrace, at the junction of Kent and Grove Roads, cost £5,000, considerably less than St Paul's, a quarter of a century earlier. Thomas Ellis Owen bore the entire cost himself. The church was 'handsome' said William White in his 1859 *Directory,* 'in the Gothic style of the 14th century' with a tower crowned by 'an elegant and lofty spire'. An ecclesiastical district comprising the southern parts of Southsea was allotted to it in due course. It was also a perpetual curacy. The patronage, however, remained in the hands of the founder.

Stewart's intransigence meant that only four new parishes were established between 1851 and his death in 1878. However by the end of the 19th century and the beginning of the 20th century, a network of church buildings

94   Pupils of St Luke's Boys' School early in the 1900s.

did exist covering Portsea Island. The combined efforts of the three strands of 19th-century Anglican churchmanship all played their part: the Evangelists, the Ritualists and the Anglican *via media*.

Two new Evangelical parishes were established in the 1860s: St Luke's and St Simon's. St Luke's Church was built in Greetham Street in a predominantly working-class district known then as Marylebone. Its neo-Norman church designed by Thomas Hellyer was built between 1858 and 1861 and would have drawn members of its congregation from the working-class areas of Southsea to the south. A remarkable Evangelical ministry was exercised here by the Aldwell family, father and son, for over sixty years. The first incumbent, Basil Aldwell, a staunch Protestant, established the tradition and served the parish for nearly forty years. His son succeeded him

in 1895, only resigning in 1920. Basil Aldwell was particularly interested in education and, when he died, the parish schools had over a thousand children on their registers and enjoyed an enviable reputation. Aldwell also established a soup kitchen, a visiting society for the relief of the poor, youth groups, branches of the Band of Hope and Scripture Union, an industrial society and a mother's meeting. He also persuaded a number of the town's leading citizens to interest themselves in the work, most notably the Pink family, grocers and local politicians.

St Simon's was a much more middle-class parish which has maintained its evangelical ministry to the present day. It is debatable whether Southsea needed another parish church quite so near to St Jude's Church but when St Simon's was built it offered a brand of churchmanship which was quite distinct from

St Jude's. A temporary church was erected initially—the 'crinoline' church, purchased from St Bartholomew's in 1862 for £200 and erected some 50 yards north of the present church. The permanent church, described by Pevsner as 'seaside "low church"' was, like St Luke's, designed by Thomas Hellyer, 1864-6. The first vicar, Frederick Baldey, a former curate of St Jude's, also established a very similar pattern of activities to St Luke's. A mission church was opened in Albert Road with regular weekday prayer meetings. An industrial society was formed to provide needlework for poor women during the winter months, a blanket and coal society and a soup kitchen. Members of the congregation at St Simon's were encouraged to buy soup tickets to give to beggars rather than money. Baldey also built the *Victoria and Albert* Temperance Tavern at 76 Albert Road where coffee and temperance literature were available. He was also very keen on revivalist meetings and during the summer months

he conducted regular services on the beach for both residents and summer visitors. He was also one of those who supported the call for the meeting at the Portland Hall on 17 December 1877 to discuss the parlous condition of the local roads which after heavy rain were often impassable round St Simon's.

There was certainly support for what might be called ritualist causes in Southsea. The Rev. Charles Kingsley, the author of *Westward Ho*, *The Waterbabies* and *Hereward the Wake*, preached two sermons at St Jude's in 1871 to raise funds for Reginald Shutte's work at the Mission of the Good Shepherd in White's Row, Portsea, one of the most socially deprived parts of that area, behind the Hard. Shutte was Thomas Platt's curate at Holy Trinity, Portsea. Platt is usually regarded as Portsmouth's first ritualist. The pattern of parish teaching, visiting and care for the poor and deprived which he established did not differ markedly from that of his Evangelical counterparts and it could be

95 St Simon's Church in Southsea, *c.*1910.

96 St Jude's Church in Southsea, *c.*1910.

97 St Peter's Church, Southsea. The original iron church of 1870 stands alongside the present church of 1882.

argued that the congregation at St Jude's were supporting this work and not the cause itself. However St Jude's was one of the first churches in Portsmouth to develop a full choral service and by the 1880s was perceived as 'Ritualistic' by some observers.

The ritualist cause was best served in Southsea at St Matthew's under the colourful leadership of its first vicar, Bruce Cornford, who was a great admirer of Robert Dolling and his work at St Agatha's, Landport. Cornford came to Portsmouth in 1897 as vicar-designate to the mission of St Matthew in the predominantly working-class district of Southsea along Fawcett Road, then part of the parish of St Bartholomew. Cornford was a great ritualist and self-publicist and, within only a few months of his arrival, was pulling huge congregations into his small mission church. A permanent church, designed by T.J. Micklethwaite, was consecrated in 1903 although it was not completed until 1924. Cornford continued to attract huge congregations to St Matthew's throughout the 1920s and 1930s with his unique brand of high churchmanship which managed to be both anti-Protestant and anti-Roman Catholic. He espoused a range of causes in the town from women's suffrage to Portsmouth Football Club, whose chairman he became in due course. The ritualist momentum,

however, was not sustained. By the 1940s the once-thriving ritualist churches on Portsea Island—St Agatha's, St Michael's and Holy Trinity—and in Southsea, St Matthew's were only half-full. Cornford died in 1940, just months before St Matthew's, like St Paul's, was destroyed on the night of 10-11 January 1941. After the war the diocese decided to unite the two parishes of St Bartholomew's and St Matthew's. St Matthew's was reconstructed to house the two congregations and rededicated—to the Holy Spirit. The restoration was carried out by S.E. Dykes Bower between 1956 and 1958 and even Pevsner was moved by the beauty of its interior. Its particular brand of high churchmanship still draws a congregation from across the city.

St Peter's Southsea and St Margaret's Eastney, both on Southsea's fringes, can also trace their descent from ritualist traditions. The churchmanship of St Peter's Southsea was comparatively moderate initially but became more ritualistic. By 1870, St Jude's was serving an area of some 11,000 people and the parish resolved in 1871 to set up a mission church—St Peter's—in Somers Town, in a temporary building on the corner of Somers Road and Baileys Lane, now Fraser Road. The congregation outgrew this structure and in 1879 a committee was set up to raise the necessary money for a new building. The foundation stone of the present church was laid in 1882. It was designed by a local architect, Alfred Hudson, of Kent Road. It is a dignified building of red brick with stone dressings and with its ancillary buildings contributes significantly to both the townscape and the daily life of its local community.

St Margaret's, like St Peter's, began life as a mission church—St Columba's Mission—in 1899. The foundation stone of the present church was laid in 1902 and the church was consecrated in 1903. Pevsner found the outside 'not very exciting' but he describes the interior as 'a church of character, quirky but success-fully so, in a more or less Bristolian Perp style'.

The Anglican *via media* or 'middle of the road' brand of churchmanship was exemplified in Southsea in Joseph Blake's period of office as vicar of St Jude's from 1869 to 1909. It was a predominantly middle-class parish—a 'carriage' church—although by the late 19th to early 20th centuries a high proportion of properties in the parish were boarding houses and it was indeed the church of the resort. Today it ranks as one of the most successful evangelical churches in the city but it acquired this reputation only in the 1930s when Bishop Ingham was appointed vicar. James Richard Cox, baker, of Marmion Road recorded in his diary on 22 May 1870 'that the practices at this Church [St Jude's] are becoming more and more Ritualistic'. He also noted earlier in this diary that Mr. Blake, who had been senior curate at St Jude's before he succeeded Mr. Brownrigg as incumbent, 'was presented with the Incumbency in answer to a memorial from the majority of the Congregation on the 4th May 1869—by Mrs. Brownrigg and the Rev. J.B. Owen the Trustees'. Mrs. Brownrigg was Thomas Ellis Owen's only child and sole heir. His son-in-law, the Rev. J. R. Brownrigg, was the first incumbent.

St Bartholomew's in Outram Road was also fairly 'middle of the road'. Carved out of Milton parish, it was built on land given by the developer of New Southsea who doubtless hoped the new church would help sell his properties. The first St Bartholomew's was the famous 'crinoline' church. It was erected in 1858 at a cost of £800 and seated 550. It looked just like a large crinoline. It was built of wood and had 20 sides which rose to an apex with a lantern. The foundation stone of the permanent church was laid in 1861 and it was consecrated in 1862. It was not a particularly beautiful building and few people mourned its demolition in 1958 when the parishes of St Bartholomew's and St Matthew's were combined and housed in the re-built St Matthew's.

98 The Crinoline Church on its final site in Portsmouth at Eastney.

Local nonconformists moved into the new suburb of Southsea before the established church. The Baptists, who were particularly strong locally, built a small chapel in Great Southsea Street in 1815, the timber for the roof, pews and wainscoting reportedly coming from a French vessel captured in the recent wars. Their most important church in Southsea, however, was the Elm Grove Chapel which opened in 1881. It was a prominent local landmark which was destroyed on the night of 10-11 January 1941. The Bible Christians, from 1907 United Methodist, were particularly active, building chapels in Little Southsea Street in 1822, Grosvenor Street in 1847, Albert Road in 1867, Brougham Road in 1876 and Fawcett Road in 1893. The Primitive Methodists followed behind with a not dissimilar distribution of chapels: the Zoar Chapel in Wellington Street in 1851, Somers Road in 1861 and Albert Road in 1875. The Wesleyan Methodists built two major churches in Southsea. The Victoria Road Church, built in 1878, was probably the wealthiest. Its congregation included a number of prosperous Southsea families. The church was demolished in the 1970s and the site sold for development. Only the Albert Road Church, now Trinity Methodist Church, survives to remind observers of the strength of the Wesleyans in 19th-century Southsea. The original church was a small iron building constructed in 1892. In 1897 the decision was made to build a larger, permanent church which opened in 1901. It was designed by a Wesleyan, R.J. Winnicott. The slender angle tower of brick with stone dressings is a local landmark. The interior is a remarkable late 19th-century survival.

Vying with the Wesleyans in Victoria Road for the support of fashionable nonconformist Southsea was Christchurch Congregational Church on the corner of Ashburton Road and Kent Road. Like the Baptists, they were strong in Portsmouth. The first small church was built in 1865 in Ashburton Road but the congregation grew so rapidly that a large new church was built in 1871. Like St Jude's, at the other end of the road, Christchurch was a 'carriage' church. It was badly damaged during the last war and was eventually demolished.

A Roman Catholic church was opened in Saxe-Weimar, after 1914 Waverley, Road in 1884. Dedicated to Our Lady and St Swithun, the original iron church soon proved too small for its congregation and a new church was built on the site which opened in 1901. The Southsea Citadel of the Salvation Army was located nearby in Albert Road. It opened in 1897 and could seat 750 people. There was another Salvation Army hall in Hyde Park Road.

A Jewish burial ground was purchased in Lazy Lane, now Fawcett Road, Southsea in 1749. The exact whereabouts of the local synagogue is only conjectural. There is some evidence to suggest that from 1732 it was in a room in a rented house in Oyster Street in the old town; the very purchase of the burial ground would seem to indicate that there was an established Jewish community in Portsmouth. But the earliest documented source survives only from 1780: a lease which confirms that there was a synagogue in White's Row, Portsea in a converted house—and that it had been in existence for some time. The house was demolished now and a purpose-built synagogue constructed. This building remained in use until 1936 when the community moved to its present site in The Thicket, Southsea.

There has been a fair amount of reorganisation, consolidation and redevelopment across the assorted religious denominations since the last war but an impressive network of churches and chapels still remains to address the spiritual needs of the people of Southsea. Most recently, the Jammi Mosque in Marmion Road, Southsea has been established for local Shia and Sunni Moslem families and a Sikh Temple in Margate Road for the Sikh community, to serve the needs of Southsea's latest incomers.

Chapter Eight

'The Gem of England's Watering Places'

When the Southsea Improvement Association agreed to write to the Town Council and congratulate them for finally putting in hand the necessary repairs to roads and footpaths in Southsea they took the opportunity to draw the council's attention

> to the necessity of many further improvements which are required to be carried out, before the Watering Place can become as attractive to Visitors as other South Coast towns—and the absence of which are the subject of daily comment and complaint by those Residents and others who live in Southsea.

They wanted asphalt laid for about 1,000 yards either side of the South Parade Pier on the raised portion of the promenade. Visitors and invalids, in their invalid carriages presumably, found it quite impossible to use these parts of the Esplanade after heavy rain as the ground remained saturated and the water lay in pools for many hours after a downpour. Other watering places of any importance had asphalted promenades along their beaches. They cited Ryde, Ventnor, Eastbourne, Hastings, Brighton and St Leonards as examples. Public seats should also be provided on the Esplanade between Southsea Castle and Lumps Fort. The towns cited had them 'in large numbers'. They drew the council's attention to the large area of loose shingle at the eastern end of Southsea Common and suggested it might be covered over with mould or 'road-scrapings' from time

99 The Pier, Parade, Baths and Assembly Rooms in 1877.

100 The Parade and Beach in 1877.

101 Southsea Castle in 1876.

to time at little or no expense to the council and would soon become as smooth and green as other parts of the Common. The Association also felt that the roadways around Southsea Common and along parts of the Terraces were too narrow for significant carriage traffic which, they said, was 'constantly remarked upon by visitors'. They believed the War Department might be induced to give up 10 or 15 feet of land in front of the Terraces to form a wider road.

Public lighting was also still an issue. The lighting 'in the front Marine terraces', presumably along the building line of Southsea Terrace, Western Parade, Clarence Parade and South Parade, was described as 'very insufficient' and it was said that, in the winter, 'it is difficult in the darkness between the lamps to pass to and fro'. Again, the council was advised that visitors would be deterred by any failure on its part to get to grips with this particular matter. The Association was also keen to see trees planted along 'the Marine Terraces'. They were very impressed by the road widening and tree planting programme implemented in other parts of the borough and would like to see a similar programme implemented in Southsea 'so that Southsea may be rendered as attractive as the other parts of the Borough'. Other complaints related to the number of ditches which existed alongside many roads which posed particular problems for visitors who kept carriages and were prevented from taking houses in Southsea 'because of the want of good

Carriage Drives'. Raised footpaths were still an issue which 'are to be seen in all other Towns, especially all over the Suburb of Southampton'. A pond, on the western side of Lumps Fort, was also causing complaints. The smell was offensive and the Association hoped that, before the weather became too hot and sultry, it could be filled in.

Water carts were another issue. They have disappeared from Portsmouth's streets since asphalt became the normal road-covering but, before, they were vital to lay the dust of unmade-up roads in dry weather. The Association complained of a complete absence of such carts. 'On the front Terraces between Clarence Esplanade and *Beach Mansion Hotel* and as far as Festing Road', it thundered, 'not one Water Cart has this year been used, and the clouds of dust at times have been most disagreeable.' They felt that the neglect was not intentional but due to the fact that Southsea was too far away from the council's depot. They suggested that an additional depot be established at Southsea. A general anxiety about their relative distance from the municipal centre also prompted the Association to express the hope that in the Town Council's current negotiations to obtain land for a new Town Hall they bear in mind the town's rapid extension eastwards and the need to choose a site in a central part of the borough. They also hoped:

that the Town Council will exhibit the greatest economy in any plans or designs for its erection, and that it will not be commenced until all the Sanitary and other Improvements ... which are so necessary for the health of the Inhabitants of Southsea are completed.

The local population currently numbered some 40,000. It was anticipated that in ten years' time it would number some 60,000. The sanitary works were vital. The Association offered these observations 'in the most friendly spirit' and hoped that the Town Council would give them due weight and consideration.

Whether or not it was pressure from the Southsea Improvement Association which prompted the Town Council to begin tackling these issues, it is difficult to judge. The council had certainly been handicapped by the fact that it had no real lien on Southsea Common. It was War Department property and where things had been achieved it had been only with the War Department's co-operation and, usually, assistance. However in 1884 the council finally obtained a lease of the land and could begin developing Southsea more easily as a resort.

The Ladies Mile was laid out and became a popular promenade after Sunday morning church. Trees were planted at long last between Pier Road and Western Parade. The ornamental garden was laid out now in front of South Parade. Also, to the delight of the residents of

102   Promenading along Ladies Mile.

Craneswater Park, the council turned to the offensive pond, drawn to their attention by the Southsea Improvement Association, 'a dismal-looking depression, strewn with rusty tins, mouldy rubbish, and other abominations', as W.G. Gates described it. Once part of the Great Morass, the War Department did in fact offer it to the Town Council some years previously, a fact clearly unknown to the Southsea Improvement Association. However, once the council discovered what it would cost to reclaim, they declined to proceed with the offer. As the lessees of the Common, it was now a different matter. It was resolved to turn the offensive pond into an ornamental lake and in 1886 it opened as the Canoe Lake, constructed by T.P. Hall to the designs of the Borough Engineer, H.P. Boulnois. It cost £3,000. The Common was also extended westwards in this year when Pembroke Gardens, on the former King's Bastion, were leased from the War Office, providing welcome recreation space beneath the elm trees for the inhabitants of the old town. Finally, in 1891, the council appointed a Parks and Open Spaces Committee which would be responsible for these newly-developed areas.

Two major disasters took place in the early years of the new century. On 8 December 1901, the *Queen's Hotel* was destroyed by fire, and two of the hotel chambermaids were killed in the flames. A few years later on 19 July 1904, South Parade Pier was partially destroyed by fire. The *Queen's Hotel* was rebuilt immediately to designs by T.W. Cutler and reopened in 1903. The pier remained derelict for some time before the Town Council decided to take matters in hand. They bravely purchased the enterprise from its owners and rebuilt it on a much grander scale. The new pier, designed by C.W. Ball, was 500 feet long. It opened on 12 August 1908. It cost £70,000. It was a few years before the council saw significant returns for its outlay but in due course it became one of the resort's greatest attractions. 1908 was in fact a year which saw conspicuous civic expenditure. Not only was the new pier opened but also the Municipal College, which cost £120,000, two new refuse destructors at £29,000, a new cemetery at £18,000, a Workhouse annexe at £27,000 and Copnor Bridge at £12,000: facilities for the whole town. While these facilities were not likely to be of any interest to the average visitor to the

103   The demolition of King's Bastion in the mid-1870s.

104 Clarence Esplanade and beach in the 1890s.

105 & 106 *Queen's Hotel* after it had been destroyed by fire in 1901.

107 The new *Queen's Hotel*, seen here in 1949, was rebuilt in 1903.

108 Postcard showing South Parade Pier 'Before it was burnt down' in 1904.

109 South Parade Pier seen here on fire on 19 July 1904.

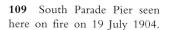

110-112 The new South Parade Pier in 1908.

113 The new South Parade Pier in 1908.

114 The Turkish Baths, King's Terrace, early in the 20th century.

resort, it is a fact that other facilities which existed to serve local residents did attract the visitors, such as the Portsmouth Swimming Club and the Southsea Rowing Club. There were also Turkish baths, established in King's Terrace, on the corner of Gold Street, in 1875 and continuing in business until 1936, when demolished to make way for Princes House.

For the more seriously minded, there was the Portsmouth and Portsea Literary and Philosophical Society, established in 1815. It had its own premises in the old town on the corner of St Mary's Street and King Street with a lecture room, a museum and a library of 1,300 volumes. The museum had a large collection of curiosities and specimens 'in every department of natural history'. Lectures were delivered or papers read on scientific subjects every Friday evening from October to March. Although it was essentially a private museum, members of the public were admitted until the society had to dissolve itself in 1860 and its collections were dispersed. There were a number of subscription libraries, the most notable being the

Hampshire Library, situated originally in St George's Square, and later, Ordnance Row, Portsea, established in 1805 by a society of shareholders. By 1859 it had more than 12,000 volumes and two 'commodious' reading rooms supplied with magazines and reviews. Other libraries included Mr. Griffin's circulating library in St James's Street and a number of smaller establishments, principally in the High Street. There was also a library at the King's Rooms. They were popular local meeting places. Places for more frivolous amusement by the middle of the century included the Theatre Royal in Landport which had opened in 1855 and several public halls which were fitted up for balls and concerts: the Beneficial Society's hall in Portsea, the Green Row Rooms in Portsmouth, the Queen's Rooms in Lion Terrace and St George's Hall in St George's Square. The King's Rooms were also the scene of a number of splendid balls and entertainments as was the *Portland Hall* after 1861. As for

gentlemen's clubs, the Prince of Wales' Clubhouse, 'large and well-furnished', stood in the High Street. It had 100 members in 1859 including many gentlemen and naval and military officers 'of the borough and neighbourhood'. On 30 September 1907, Southsea's own theatre, the King's Theatre, opened with H.B. Irving, one of Sir Henry Irving's sons, appearing in *The Lyons Mail*, *The Bells* and *Charles the First*.

Southsea's shops also provided attractions for visitors to the resort. The main shopping area was confined to just three streets: Palmerston Road, Osborne Road and Marmion Road. By the end of the 19th century, Palmerston Road and its neighbouring streets boasted a range of shops which astounds the reader a hundred years later. In Palmerston Road itself branches of the major banks, Capital and Counties, the National Provincial and Grant and Maddison's Union Banking Company stood alongside early department

115 Palmerston Road in 1876, looking north towards St Jude's Church and Grove Road.

116 Palmerston Road looking north, *c.*1910, from Handley's Corner.

117 Palmerston Road looking south from St Jude's Church, 1902.

118 Handley's Corner in the 1920s.

119 Handley's Corner, decorated for the Silver Jubilee of King George V in 1935.

120 Handley's Corner in 1939.

121 Looking towards Osborne Road from the junction of Palmerston Road in the 1930s.

122 Elm Grove in 1911.

stores Knight and Lee at Nos 25–33 Palmerston Road, J.D. Morant's at Nos 47–49 and George Handley at Nos 54–64. Grocers included William Pink and Sons at No. 5 Palmerston Road and Frank Whitcomb at No. 122. There were court dressmakers, milliners, costumiers, butchers, cooks and confectioners, fishmongers and wine and spirit merchants. Osborne Road, of course, had a considerable number of lodging houses at its western end but towards Palmerston Road there was a fine range of different trades and activities: ironmongers, booksellers, photographers, antique furniture dealers, an artist, fruiterers and greengrocers, tailors and a portmanteau maker, several tea rooms and public houses, butchers, cycle manufacturers and hairdressers. Marmion Road had a similar range of trades but in place of the lodging houses were two private hotels, a Conservative Club, St Jude's Mission Chapel, a marble mason, several registries for servants,

a bookbinders and Edwin John Brewer, tea expert and post office. These were the shops patronised by both visitors and the local élite, and the rateable values of these properties reflected their economic importance. There was a modest shopping area in King's Road which was moving slowly eastwards by the end of the 19th century and swallowing up the gardens of the leafy villas of Elm Grove, but this development never achieved the importance of the Marmion Road, Palmerston Road, Osborne Road axis.

H.G. Wells was a draper's assistant at Hyde's Emporium in nearby King Street from 1881–3. He was not particularly happy there but he put the experience to good use in at least two of his novels, *Kipps*, and *The History of Mr. Polly*. It would be very interesting to know how many of his Southsea experiences Sir Arthur Conan Doyle put into his novels. He set up in practice at 1, Bush Villas, Elm

123 'On the Parade, Southsea', 1893, from the *Illustrated London News*. Probably on the seaward side of Southsea Castle.

124   Whitmonday cartoon, Portsmouth, 1892.

125   Clarence Pier, *c.*1900.

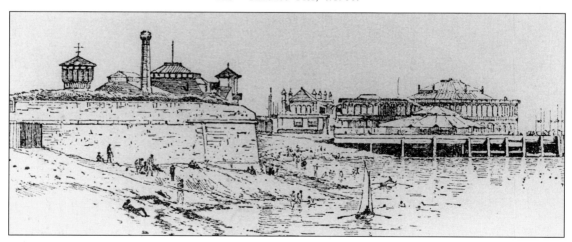

Grove in 1882 and it was there that four of his best-known novels were written, *A Study in Scarlet*, *Micah Clarke*, *The White Company* and *The Sign of Four* and where, of course, Sherlock Holmes was born. Dr. Doyle also took an active part in local society. In the 1880s he played cricket and bowls and was a founder-member of Portsmouth Football Club. He also joined the Literary and Scientific Society, one of whose members was a Dr. Watson, and he married a girl he met in Southsea, Miss Louise Hawkins, in 1885.

By the turn of the century Southsea was a substantial middle-class suburb. The tourist trade was also an important local industry. The Southsea and Portsmouth Entertainment Committee was formed in 1905. It was not a council initiative although it consisted mainly of council members. The committee undertook to provide all the equipment necessary 'to add to the attractions of Southsea' such as chairs, bandstands, artists and performers. Other new attractions included a miniature golf course opened in 1914 at the eastern end of the sea front and new bowling greens at the Canoe Lake. The whole enterprise prospered marvellously and, under the 1920 Corporation Act, powers were obtained to take over the Entertainment Committee, its assets and liabilities as a going concern and its business was taken forward by the council's newly-constituted Beach and Publicity Committee. The authors of the 1919 *Guide* felt that they could claim with some justification that Southsea was now 'the gem of England's watering places'.

126   Clarence Pier Approach in 1905.

Chapter Nine

'Sunny Southsea'

The 1920s and 1930s were hey-days of Southsea as a resort. Excursionists on cheap-day returns and family holiday makers staying in the local hotels and boarding houses crammed 'Sunny Southsea' during the summer months, particularly at Bank Holiday times and for special events. Bowling, lawn tennis, sailing and swimming, pitch and putt, bands on the pier and at the bandstand and summer shows—all were there to beguile the summer visitor.

The Council finally purchased Southsea Common from the War Department in 1922 and set about spending large sums of money— some £60,000—on converting it into gardens and recreation areas. Grass and hard tennis courts were constructed, bowling greens, putting courses and football and lacrosse pitches. According to Gates, this proved a very popular improvement, 'as during the seasons 1927 and 1928, thousands of persons enjoyed healthy recreation by participating in these various sports'.

Ornamental gardens were laid out on the site of the Ladies Mile during the winters of 1924 and 1925. They were not laid out in any definitive style. The aim was to obtain maximum shelter and use minimum soil. This last was desperately important. As Gates put it pithily, 'from a horticultural stand-point, it [the Common] was a miniature Sahara', a hundred acres of shingle almost destitute of soil. The Corporation staff perse-vered, however, and, although the choicest specimens did not thrive in these harsh conditions, the gardens did prosper and were rated by both visitors and residents to rank favourably alongside other comparable seaside resorts and inland spas and even continental venues.

127-30 The Rock Gardens, South Parade Gardens, Bowling Greens and Tennis Courts in the 1920s.

So successful was the venture that more gardens were established in succeeding winters and considerable effort was put into improving the quality of the grass adjoining these new beds. The result, said Gates:

> provides a most attractive rendezvous for all sections of the community as sheltered nooks are provided where the aged and infirm may gain repose, and ample opportunity is provided for those who are fond of games, while those who love music may enjoy the bands which play regularly in a bandstand of unique design.

He described further in *Records of the Corporation* work which began in the late 1920s on rock gardens 'which for size will rival any that have been artificially constructed in Great Britain'. The aim was to provide shelter from the cold winds 'which are occasionally felt in all seaside resorts'. Aviaries in the banks of rock were planned 'so that bird lovers will be enabled to study and admire the gaily plumaged birds of foreign origin, as well as to enjoy the sweet cadence of the birds of our native land which

frequent the gardens'. A paddling pool for children was built on the west side of Southsea Castle with raised seats alongside for those in charge of the children. W.G. Gates summed up the achievements as developments which should satisfy a wide range of tastes and interests: 'the horticulturist, the bird lover, and those who enjoy modern games ... a garden of pleasure for all ages ...'.

Standing sentinel over these developments and a poignant memorial to recent sacrifices as well as a reminder to visitors of Portsmouth's first role as home of the Royal Navy, was the Royal Naval War Memorial on the Clarence Esplanade. It was unveiled by the Duke of York, later King George VI, on 15 October 1924. Erected to honour the 9,300 officers and men of the Portsmouth Division of the Royal Navy who died in the Great War of 1914–18, it was designed by Sir Robert Lorimer. It is an elegant monument of a tapering square column on a plinth with pedestals surmounted by lions placed diagonally at the corners. 'Surveying this', said a contemporary

131 The Paddling Pool at Southsea Castle.

Guide, 'which is a land-mark for ships making harbour, let it be remembered that Portsmouth, the home of the Navy, has ever been the first in time of war to suffer loss and bereavement.'

The terms of the purchase of Southsea Common in 1922 did in fact stipulate that part of the Common west of a line drawn from the western angle of Southsea Castle to the *Grosvenor Hotel* had to be preserved as open space, so as to be available for military operations. As Gates reminded his readers, it was still an area 'where the armed forces of England may be trained to prepare for any national emergency and where on State and special occasions magnificent parades and reviews of troops may be admired'.

Southsea Castle itself was an important part of the 'Fortress Portsmouth' scheme in the years leading up to the outbreak of the First World War. This scheme encompassed the vital defence of both Portsmouth and Southampton. When war broke out in 1914, the castle's guns were manned by regular Royal Garrison Artillery and by No. 4 (Portsmouth)

Company of the Hampshire R.G.A. Territorials. During 1915, however, the men of the No. 4 Company were drafted abroad in increasing numbers and by 1917 the guns had been handed over to 'citizen artillerists' of the newly-formed Hampshire R.G.A. Volunteers. Happily no enemy seaborne threat materialised.

The 1928 season was the most successful on record. The previous year there were 6,898 applications for guide books and lists of hotels. This year there were applications from 16,900 enquirers. This enormous increase was put down to the bold advertising programme of the Beach and Publicity Committee. The number of personal enquiries at the Publicity Office also vastly exceeded those of any previous season and staff were immensely heartened by the very positive comments of visitors on the improvements undertaken over the previous few years. The weather also exceeded all hopes and expectations. There was a good May followed by a somewhat indifferent June but thereafter there were four glorious months: weeks of brilliant sunshine, the heat tempered

132   The Avenue, Ladies Mile, in the late 1920s.

133   South Parade in 1932.

by the sea breeze. Never had the appellation 'Sunny Southsea' been so well deserved. From late May until the end of August there was also a continuous succession of galas and sports. Major events included a Civic Week with a battle of flowers and illuminations, a Children's Week and a Navy Week. So successful were these special weeks that it was resolved that they should become a feature of the programmes of activity in future years. There was an excess of income over expenditure at the end of the season of just over £7,000 and this was ploughed back into winter expenditure and preparation for the 1929 season.

The 1929 *Official Guide* speaks proudly of the Corporation's achievements in the making of Southsea Common 'the greatest pleasure garden on the south coast'. The opening paragraphs set the tone:

> Steeped in traditions of the past envisaging the naval pageantry of the present, and sheltered by England's most lovely isle, there has arisen in the centre of the southern coast a great seaside health and pleasure resort—Southsea.

Apart from her nearness to the home of the Navy for a thousand years, and to that unique memorial, Nelson's *Victory*, a lasting heritage of the nation, Southsea can justly lay claim to all those desirable things which attract the footsteps of those who seek holiday.

Variety, the author assured readers, was here in abundance 'and all so near to London'. Variety there was undoubtedly. Few resorts could boast heavy gun practice as one of its attractions. Southsea Castle, the *Guide* informed its readers, was still in the occupation of the military authorities, and at frequent intervals heavy gun practice took place from the ramparts. 'To those who have never observed ranging and firing at sea targets, the spectacle is of some interest, particularly as the conformation of the Esplanade allows close approach to the guns; and from the tea house, situate behind the Castle on its landward side, the gun's crew can be seen operating.' Built by the Corporation, the tea house faced the bandstand. It was approached by rock gardens, the writer said, which in spring and summer were ablaze with colour, and was placed at the centre

134 South Parade tea house in the 1930s.

135   Swan boats at Canoe Lake in the late 1920s.

of the many recent improvements to the Common.

The Beach and Publicity Committee were clearly enchanted when the French novelist, André Maurois, paid tribute to Southsea in a broadcast of his children's impressions of England during a tour of the country. They visited HMS *Victory* and then proceeded to Southsea. The high point was the Canoe Lake. Never, said the distinguished author, had his children seen anything they liked so much. The youngest wrote that night to his grandmother in France:

> We like England very much. It is very beautiful. We have seen Salisbury Cathedral which is very fine and the ship where Nelson died which is all gold with wooden guns, and Westminster Abbey where they crown the kings of England and the Tower, where they cut their heads off. But the best things in England are the tin canoes at Southsea.

More publicity was secured in 1929 when on 7 September the great sea plane contest for the Schneider Trophy took place on the stretch of sea between Southsea and the Isle of Wight. Stands were erected along the sea front to accommodate viewers and extra car parks and lavatory accommodation organised. Half-a-million people were expected. As it turned out, this proved to be an over-optimistic assessment of likely numbers and the Corporation was put to much needless expense. The beach and esplanade offered ample—free—accommodation for sightseers who thronged the beaches from end to end, standing twenty to fifty deep. Victory was secured for Britain by Flying Officer Waghorn at a speed of 328.63 miles per hour.

Earlier in the year, on 24 July, the Portsmouth Horticultural Society held its first summer show on Southsea Common and attracted both exhibits and visitors from far and wide. More sadly it was recorded that in 1929 the last of the elm trees in Elm Grove was pulled down.

The following year sand pits, swings 'and other entrancing devices' for children were installed round the Castle paddling pool. The carriageway along the sea front was also remade to form a drive way suitable now for motor cars. The Beach and Publicity Committee took the unusual step of producing a *Guide* free from advertisements. They received applications for the book from all parts of the country and distributed some 33,000 copies. Each enquirer was also sent a panorama of Portsmouth and Southsea by the marine artist, W.L. Wyllie R.A., who lived in the old town. They became collectors' pieces. Complaints about bad lighting now became a thing of the past. This season over 9,000 lamps were festooned from Clarence Pier to South Parade Pier, along

the Parades themselves and round the Canoe Lake.

Southsea's merits as a winter resort were celebrated in 1931 by Dr. A. Mearns Fraser in his Annual Report. Referring to its rapid development as a popular seaside resort, the doctor suggested that the mildness of the climate and large amount of sunshine rendered it particularly beneficial to the old and those in delicate health 'and for those reasons it is becoming increasingly appreciated as a winter resort'.

An interesting debate on Sunday restrictions took place in the early 1930s. Such restrictions seem incomprehensible today but throughout the 1930s Sundays in Southsea were quiet events, dull and often dreary. The Piers, Beach and Publicity Committee, as it was now called, decided to enter the fray. Children secured permission to use the paddling pool and ride on the miniature railway first but only

136   Southsea Illuminations in 1930.

137   Mrs. Grundy!

not withdrawn and the Piers, Beach and Publicity Committee congratulated itself on an excellent publicity coup.

The highlight of 1935, on 16 July, was King George V's Jubilee Naval Review. A major programme of events had marked the actual anniversary on 6 May. The Corporation penned a loyal address. There was also a thanksgiving service in the Guildhall Square. The Lord Mayor presided and the Bishop of Portsmouth delivered an address. There were lavish street parties and, at the end of the week's celebrations, 25,000 children were admitted free to local cinemas. On the night of 6 May there were fireworks on Portsdown Hill and at 10 p.m. a great bonfire was lit, one of a number of similar beacons across the country. There was also a splendid Jubilee Ball. These were

after heated debate in the council chamber when one member remarked that certain of his colleagues seemed to regard the miniature railway as a mainline railway to hell. A much more bitter debate took place on whether or not local cinemas should be allowed to open on Sundays. It was put to a vote of the local inhabitants who found in favour of the proposal by a handsome majority. Later in the year, it was resolved to open public recreation grounds for sporting activities on what, for many workers, was their only day off in the week. Delighted with their success, the Piers, Beach and Publicity Committee decided to capitalise upon it. They issued a poster showing 'Mrs. Grundy' with her bag of troubles departing the resort which was now declared free of all restrictions. 'Southsea for Sundays', the poster declared. Golf, tennis, croquet, bowls, flying and cinemas were all now available. Unfortunately a section of the local community, led by a Southsea vicar, demanded the poster's withdrawal on the grounds that it was an 'invitation to all manner of improprieties and unbridled licence'. The *contretemps* made national newspaper headlines but the poster was

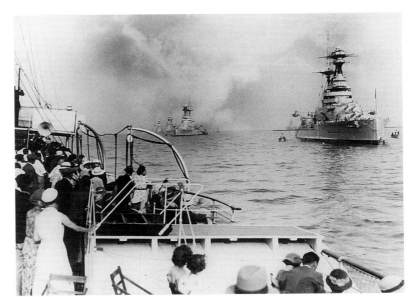

138 & 139   King George V's Jubilee Naval Review in 1935.

local celebrations, though. The Review was a national celebratory event and it took place in Portsmouth. The weather on the day was magnificent and the city was in party mood. Tens of thousands of visitors filled the seafront. There were 27 miles of ships: ships of the Royal Navy, the Merchant Service and the Fishing Fleet. At night each vessel was outlined with electric lamps and red flares were held aloft by thousands of sailors. At a signal from the Royal Yacht, the flares were extinguished by throwing them into the sea. Bouquets of rockets then hurtled into the sky from each ship. This was followed by a display in which 500 search-lights swept the night skies. The spectacle thrilled to the core the onlookers on the shore.

The City Council purchased Lumps Fort in 1932, as much to save it from being developed as a funfair as for any other reason. A design competition was launched in 1935 to encourage innovative thinking on the area's development. The first prize was won by Wesley Dougill and E.A. Ferriby of Liverpool but their scheme was not proceeded with. Another scheme was devised by the City Architect, which would have involved closing the road along the sea front and creating a 40-ft. promenade, while on the land side of the fort a 90-ft. wide tree-lined boulevard was planned, made by widening Eastern Parade. There would be two 30-ft. wide carriageways.

Cumberland House was to be demolished and a new roadway constructed linking Festing Road with the sea. Picturesque ornamental gardens and pools with fountains, lit at night, would be devised to flank the new roads. Bathing pools, new beaches and terraces, squash courts, badminton and table tennis facilities, a dance hall capable of accommodating 1,000 people, new tennis courts and bowling greens, car parks including at least one underground car parking facility, were all part of this splendid proposal. Brimming with confidence the Piers, Beach and Publicity Committee began to cost up their latest scheme.

Another magnificent fleet review took place at Spithead on 22 May 1937, King George VI's Coronation Review. Over 160 ships, including 17 foreign vessels, were reviewed by the king who steamed through the lines of ships in the Royal Yacht *Victoria and Albert*. The Admiralty placed the surveying ship HMS *Kellett* at the disposal of the Lord Mayor and members of the City Council to witness the spectacle and see the illuminations close at hand. It must have been a welcome—and reassuring—distraction from other more worrying matters for, since the beginning of the year, the question of the protection of the civil population against air raids in the event of war had begun to demand their serious attention.

Chapter Ten

Chill Winds

The Lumps Fort scheme was one of the first casualties in the months before the outbreak of the Second World War. As early as 26 September 1938, the Passive Air Defence Committee set up by the City Council said that work for protection of the civilian population was to take precedence over all else. At their meeting on 9 May 1939 the Council appointed three of their number to act as an Emergency Committee in matters of Civil Defence. With the Town Clerk in his capacity as Controller, this committee would have wide powers in time of war to act on behalf of the Council. Displays on Southsea Common during the summer months of 1939 included a large-scale demonstration on the evening of 7 June by Portsmouth auxiliary firemen of fire fighting methods and the spectators, who numbered well over two thousand, were able to see Air Raid Precaution (A.R.P.) fire fighting equipment in operation for the first time. On 27 July local schoolchildren took part in a major evacuation test, 900 hundred volunteering to be transported from George Street School in 14 Corporation buses to the Greetham Street goods depot for entraining at Portsmouth and Southsea.

War was declared on 3 September 1939. The city anticipated being a front-line target. All theatres and cinemas were closed immediately and football matches were stopped. The cinemas re-opened ten days later, however, and professional football two days afterwards. Life had to go on. Southsea was profoundly affected,

however, by regulations introduced on 4 July 1940 when the whole of the seafront was closed. This decision involved closing South Parade Pier and Clarence Pier, the kiosks and tea houses, the Rock Gardens, Canoe Lake and miniature golf course. On 5 July Portsmouth was declared a Defence Area. There was outrage locally. As a result of a belated conference between the civilian and military authorities, civilian access to the beach and gardens was partially restored from 7 August and before too long the stretch of beach between the western side of Southsea Castle and Clarence Pier was opened for bathing between 5 and 8 p.m. and the Canoe Lake was reopened.

The first air raid on Portsmouth took place on 11 July 1940. Parts of Southsea were hit in the second raid on 12 August. Major damage took place on the night of 10-11 January 1941, the first blitz of the city. The Palmerston Road and King's Road shopping centres were destroyed, as were Clarence Pier and the *Esplanade Hotel* among a number of other notable buildings. The Garrison Church was seriously damaged. St Paul's Church, Elm Grove Baptist Church and Immanuel Baptist Church were almost totally destroyed. During the night of 10-11 March, in the second blitz, St Matthew's Church was burnt out.

Southsea Castle had a brief moment of glory when it played a part in the taking over of the French Fleet. On 23 June 1940 the garrison received urgent orders to man its guns

140   *Above*. Palmerston Road in 1945, by V. Pearse.

141   *Right*. King's Road in 1943, by V. Pearse.

142   *Above right*. Bomb damage in King's Road, 1943.

and be ready to open fire on a number of French naval vessels which had escaped to Spithead. The French destroyer, *Leopard*, turned its guns on the Castle. There was a stand-off and in the early hours of 3 July naval boarding parties commandeered the French ships. The Prime Minister was able to tell the House of Commons on 4 July that 'measures' had been taken to prevent the French fleet falling into German hands. All told, the fleet consisted of two battleships, two light cruisers, and submarines, including one very large one, eight destroyers and roughly 200 smaller and very useful craft. They had been distributed between Portsmouth, Plymouth and Sheerness. However, it was from the air that the threat to Portsmouth came, not from the sea. The Castle itself was hit several times by incendiary bombs but the fires were put out quickly. A number of different units did tours of duty there besides coast artillery. The Home Guard also did nightly sentry duty on the ramparts. In the early hours of 20 September 1941 the Southern Railway Paddle Steamer, *Portsdown*, blew up and sank off Southsea beach, eight crew and an unknown number of passengers going missing. She was believed to have struck a mine. A former pleasure steamer, the Naval Paddle Mine Sweeper, *Lorna Doone*, had better luck. She brought down one enemy bomber and damaged another the following year for only two men wounded. Southsea Common was used by anti-aircraft gun and rocket batteries.

The Beach Trading Department of the Corporation turned its energies to supplying hot midday meals from its kitchens in Heidelberg Road to Emergency Centres where dispossessed people were received after air raids. One of the largest Municipal Restaurants in Portsmouth was in fact located in Albert Road, Southsea. It opened on 29 October 1941. It could accommodate 275 diners and was capable of feeding 1,000 a day. A three-course lunch cost 10d.

With the loss of the Guildhall on the night of 10-11 January 1941, the hunt began for alternative office accommodation for city council staff. On 11 January, the War Emergency Committee took over the *Royal Beach Hotel* which had been closed. The staff moved in the following morning. Mayor-making took place that year on South Parade Pier and the mayoral lunch at the conclusion of the ceremonies was held at the *Royal Beach*.

On 17 August 1943 at noon a ban regarding restricted areas of the South Coast came into force. All members of the public had to leave the sea front and immediate vicinity at once unless they had special permits or temporary passes. All boarding-house keepers and hotel proprietors had received warning from the police that all guests who were not in the area for approved purposes had to be out by 17 August and that no more visitors were to be accepted. Early in the following year the ban was extended for reasons which became obvious later in the year. The largest ever coastal ban came into operation on 1 April 1944 and affected a belt 10 miles deep from the Wash to Land's End. The prohibition prevented persons not resident in the affected areas on 1 April 1944 from entering or leaving those areas after that date. To ensure that the order was complied with a check would be kept at all times on railway stations and buses and other public vehicles. Checks would also be kept on hotels and boarding houses and places of entertainment and anyone discovered not carrying his or her identity card was liable to arrest on the spot. Portsmouth and Southsea had its quietest Easter holiday on record. What few local people knew was that the build up to D-Day itself was gathering momentum. Since 1943 troops had been training for the invasion of continental Europe on beaches similar to those they would expect to find in Normandy. One of the biggest exercises took place in May 1944 to test the effectiveness of the combined forces. Locally, British and Canadian troops 'invaded' Littlehampton, Bracklesham Bay and Hayling Island. Signs of impending action were also obvious in the lines of vehicles and tanks heading south, the work being done to establish inland repair bases and build and improve docking facilities and slipways. By the time the invasion forces were at last assembled, there was accommodation in place locally for 3,000 landing craft, billets for 29,000 personnel and 172,000 square feet of storage space.

During the first month of the invasion, 6 June—6 July 1944, nearly 207,000 personnel and 37,000 vehicles were loaded in the Isle of Wight area which included Stokes Bay, Southsea and Lymington. South Parade Pier was used to embark troops from a specially constructed scaffolding walkway. On 25 August the 10-mile coastal ban was lifted. The following spring, on 4 April 1945, amateur fishing, yachting and pleasure boating was resumed off Southsea beach. The resort had served its turn and played its part in the great enterprise.

The resort emerged from the trauma of the war to enjoy a flourishing decade of activity. It was now, in fact, the municipal centre. Corporation departments had taken up residence in a number of former hotels and apartment buildings on Western Parade and Clarence Parade and, though the Lord Mayor and Town Clerk moved back to the rebuilt Guildhall when it opened in 1958, other departments were not brought together again until the Civic Offices opened in 1976.

During the 1950s Southsea continued to attract large crowds of holiday makers. Pre-war favourites figure largely in the literature: the pier, the gardens, children's play facilities, the canoe lake, the ever-changing panorama of shipping. The Corporation organised an impressive range of entertainment on South Parade Pier. The 1956 season saw Jack Hylton and Chesney Allen presenting Tommy Trinder 'and great West-End cast' in 'You Lucky People'. It was billed as Southsea's finest ever resident summer show. It played twice-nightly for 12 weeks from 27 June until 15 September. Reginald Porter-Brown played his 'Wonder

143 List of Attractions including the comedian Tommy Trinder, 1956.

Hammond Concert Organ' for two hours each morning and afternoon from late April until the end of September, and each Sunday evening there were Radio Band Shows. Productions by local amateur companies, the

144   Miss Southsea in 1953.

145   Fireworks at South Parade Pier in the 1950s.

Southsea Shakespeare Actors, the Arts Theatre and the Portsmouth Players took place during May and after the closure of the resident summer show in mid-September, effectively took the programme of activity through until the end of September. There were also firework displays each Wednesday evening at 10.30p.m. and the annual Miss Southsea competition. It was a heady mixture and the shows played to packed houses. Southsea hit the headlines once again in 1958 with the Bikini Girl controversy. A poster produced jointly by the Piers, Beach and Publicity Committee and British Rail of a girl in a bikini crouching on the sands in what was construed by some as a provocative pose roused another storm of controversy. The general consensus, however, was that the poster was no bad thing and, once again, the Council cashed in on the publicity. A contest was organised to find the girl most like the painting.

146 The Southsea Bikini Girl Poster Contest, 1958.

148 Judges and Audience!

Meanwhile the rebuilding of the war-ravaged parts of the city was continuing. King's Road was not redeveloped as a shopping area. New blocks of low-rise council flats were erected here and in the adjoining streets to the north and south. Palmerston Road was re-developed and new department stores have risen to replace those destroyed in the bombing, chief amongst them Handleys, now Debenhams, and the John Lewis department store of Knight and Lee. Many familiar names did not return, however, and changing shopping patterns have taken their toll of the independent retailers of the early years of the century in both Palmerston Road and the adjoining streets of Marmion Road and Osborne Road.

Similarly, package tours and cheap charter flights to the sun have severely diminished the traditional domestic seaside trade not only in Southsea but in the legions of similar resorts round the country which developed, like Southsea, from modest beginnings in the early to mid-19th century. Today's visitors are more likely to be day-trippers whose interests are no longer in Southsea's 'bucket and spade' traditions but in the area's naval—and military—heritage. It is this wealth of fortified emplacements and Portsmouth's unique naval history—which is where the story of Southsea begins—which brings people to the city today. Between them, local museums and heritage attractions, Portsmouth City Council's and those in the historic Naval Base, attracted just over half a million visitors in 1999-2000. This represents on its own a healthy £2.5 million at least factored into the local economy across a whole tranche of local providers.

Efforts still continue, too, to develop the range of facilities available to the traditional visitor. It is not too fanciful to suggest that the spirit which moved Mr. Henry Hollingsworth in the 1820s to build his vapour baths and assembly rooms informed the promoters of the Pyramid complex. Interestingly the new *Travel Inn* actually stands on the site of the former *Esplanade Hotel*, which itself was built on the site of the former King's Rooms. And the sea front gardens are still tended zealously by the Council's Leisure Service contractors.

Of even more interest are the residents of Southsea who donned the mantle of the former Southsea Improvement Association, the Southsea Environs Association. Distressed by what they saw as the City Council's failure to get to grips with what they perceived as particularly 'Southsea' issues, such as traffic, parking and public transport and problems associated with Southsea's high concentration of clubs and restaurants, they handed the council a petition on 6 May 1998 signed by 2,169 persons requesting that urban parish status be conferred on part of Southsea, essentially the historic resort area. The City Council subsequently commissioned MORI to assess local residents' views on, and attitudes to, the proposed establishment of a parish council. Residents were almost evenly divided on the proposal but what the survey did highlight was that four in five residents felt strongly that they belonged to Southsea. Three in five thought Southsea's needs might well be different from the rest of Portsmouth. The debate rumbles on. A parish council was established in May 1999. It cannot be said that it has yet realised its full potential as a means of influencing Southsea's direction. However, it is reassuring that there is still a body of opinion which does care keenly about the future of this watering-place and, despite the fact that there is always something to be done, some improvements which can be made, Southsea has weathered the years in much better shape than many of her former rivals on the south coast. And the City Council is still promoting a robust programme of musical and other recreational activities. On Bank Holiday Monday, 29 May 2000, Bob Geldof played the new sea front bandstand as part of the BBC's Music Live festival. There were 5,000 gathered watching, on Southsea Castle's western batteries. The concert closed with a magnificent firework display!

Select Bibliography

General

East, Robert (ed.), *Extracts from Records in the Possession of the Municipal Corporation of the Borough of Portsmouth and from Other Documents relating thereto* (1891)

Gates, William G. and successors (eds.), *City of Portsmouth. Records of the Corporation, 1835-1974*, 7 vols. (1928-83)

Gates, William G., *Illustrated History of Portsmouth* (1900)

Howell, Alexander N.Y., *Notes on the Topography of Portsmouth* (1913)

Lilley, Henry, T. and Everitt, Alfred T., *Portsmouth Parish Church* (1921)

Lloyd, David W., *Buildings of Portsmouth and its Environs* (1974)

Portsmouth Papers, The (1967-)

Portsmouth Record Series (1971-)

The Victoria History of the County of Hampshire and the Isle of Wight, 5 vols. (1900-12)

Webb, John and others (eds.), *Hampshire Studies* (1981)

Webb, John and others, *The Spirit of Portsmouth. A History* (1989)

Chapter One: Early History

Brooks, Stephen, *Southsea Castle* (1996)

Hoad, Margaret J., 'Portsmouth—As others have seen it (Part 1 1540-1790)', *P.[ortsmouth] P.[aper]* 15 (1972)

Hoad, Margaret J., 'Portsmouth—As others have seen it (Part 2 1790-1900)', *P.P.* 20 (1973)

Quail, Sarah, 'The Origins of Portsmouth and the First Charter', *P.P.* 65 (1994)

Webb, John, *The City of Portsmouth and the Royal Navy* (1984)

Webb, John, 'The Siege of Portsmouth in the Civil War', *P.P.* 7 (1969). Reprinted 1977.

Chapter Two: The New Suburb of Southsea

Allen, Lake, *The History of Portsmouth* (1817)

Hoad, Margaret J., 'Portsmouth—As others have seen it (Part 2 1790-1900)', *P.P.* 20 (1973)

Riley, R.C., 'The Growth of Southsea as a Naval Satellite and Victorian Resort', *P.P.* 16 (1972)

Webb, J. and others, *The Spirit of Portsmouth. A History* (1989)

Chapter Three: Southsea Develops

Pevsner, Nikolaus and Lloyd, David, 'Hampshire and the Isle of Wight', *The Buildings of England* (1967)

Quail, Sarah and others (eds.), *Consecrated to Prayer: A Centenary History of St Mary's, Portsea, 1889-1989* (1989)

Quail, Sarah, 'Thomas Ellis Owen's Southsea', unpublished lecture delivered to a number of local societies 1983-5, P(ortsmouth) C(ity) R(ecords) O(ffice) Information Boxes.

Rawlinson, Robert, *Report to the General Board of Health* (1850)

Riley, R.C., 'The Growth of Southsea as a Naval Satellite and Victorian Resort, *P.P.* 16 (1972)

Riley, R.C., 'The Houses and Inhabitants of Thomas Ellis Owen's Southsea', *P.P.* 32 (1980)

Webb, J. and others, *The Spirit of Portsmouth. A History* (1989)

White, William, *History, Gazetteer and Directory of Hampshire and the Isle of Wight* (1859)

Chapter Four: The Railway Comes!

Course, Edwin, 'Portsmouth Railways', *P.P.* 6 (1969; reprinted 1972)

Riley, R.C., 'Railways and Portsmouth Society 1847-1947', *P.P.* 70 (2000)

Riley R.C., 'The Growth of Southsea as a Naval Satellite and Victorian Resort', *P.P.* 16 (1972)

Webb, J. and others, *The Spirit of Portsmouth. A History* (1989)

Chapter Five: A Constantly Changing Scene at Sea

Allen, Lake, *The History of Portsmouth* (1817)

Brooks, Stephen, *Southsea Castle* (1996)

Field, J.L., 'The Battle of Southsea', *P.P.* 34 (1981)

Gates, William G. and successors (eds.), *City of Portsmouth. Records of the Corporation, 1835-1974*, 7 vols. (1928-83)

Gates, William G., *Illustrated History of Portsmouth* (1900)

Hoad, Margaret J., 'Portsmouth—As others have seen it (Part 2 1790-1900)', *P.P.* 20 (1973)

Wade, G.R., 'The Wind of Change: Naval Reviews at Spithead 1842-56', *P.P.* 49 (1987)

White, William, *History, Gazetteer and Directory of Hampshire and the Isle of Wight* (1859)

Chapter Six: Cleanliness

Gates, William G. and successors (eds.), *City of Portsmouth. Records of the Corporation, 1835-1974*, 7 vols. (1928-83)

P.C.R.O. PUS

Peacock, Sarah, 'Borough Government in Portsmouth, 1835-1974', *P.P.* 23 (1975)

Rawlinson, Robert, *Report to the General Board of Health* (1850)

Chapter Seven: Godliness

Gates, William G., *Illustrated History of Portsmouth* (1900)

Offord, John, *Churches on Portsea Island* (1989)

P.C.R.O. CHU 2

Peacock, Sarah, 'Diary of a Southsea Tradesman', *P(ortsmouth) A(rchives) R(eview)*, vol. 1 (1976)

Pevsner, Nikolaus and Lloyd, David, 'Hampshire and the Isle of Wight', *The Buildings of England* (1967)

Quail, Sarah and Wilkinson, Alan (eds.), *Forever Building. Essays to Mark the Completion of the Cathedral Church of St Thomas of Canterbury, Portsmouth* (1995)

Quail, Sarah and others (eds.), *Consecrated to Prayer: A Centenary History of St Mary's Portsea, 1889-1989* (1989)

Yates, Nigel, 'The Anglican Revival in Victorian Portsmouth', *P.P.* 37 (1983)

Chapter Eight: 'The Gem of England's Watering Places'

Gates, William G. and successors (eds.), *City of Portsmouth. Records of the Corporation, 1835-1974*, 7 vols. (1928-83)

Kelly's Directories (1996)

P.C.R.O. PUS

Riley R.C., 'The Growth of Southsea as a Naval Satellite and Victorian Resort', *P.P.* 16 (1972)

Sargeant, J., 'A History of Portsmouth Theatres', *P.P.* 13 (1971; reprinted 1979)

White, William, *History, Gazetteer and Directory of Hampshire and the Isle of Wight* (1859)

Chapter Nine: Sunny Southsea

Brooks, Stephen, *Southsea Castle* (1996)

Gates, William G. and successors (eds.), *City of Portsmouth. Records of the Corporation, 1835-1974*, 7 vols. (1928-83)

Southsea and Portsmouth. Official Guide (1929)

Chapter 10: Chill Winds

Brooks, Stephen, *Southsea Castle* (1996)

Gates, William G. and successors (eds.), *City of Portsmouth. Records of the Corporation, 1835-1974*, 7 vols. (1928-83)

Portsmouth and Southsea. Official Guide (1956)

Stedman, John, 'Portsmouth Reborn. Destruction and Reconstruction 1939-1974', *P.P.* 66 (1995)

Index

The Town Hall

POR

So

A picture postcard sent from Southsea in 1907.